Taking Responsibi
Learning and Teaching

Also available from Continuum

Developing a Self-Evaluating School, Paul K. Ainsworth

Learn to Transform, Graham Corbyn and David Crossley

Taking Responsibility for Learning and Teaching

From Principles to Practice

Chris Turner

continuum

Due to governmental changes implemented since this book was written, the author refers to certain state-funded bodies, such as the Department for Children, Schools and Families (DCSF), which no longer exist.

Continuum International Publishing Group

The Tower Building	80 Maiden Lane
11 York Road	Suite 704
London	New York
SE1 7NX	NY 10038

www.continuumbooks.com

British Library Cataloguing-in-Publication Data
A catalogue record for this book is available from the British Library.
ISBN: 978-1-8553-9785-9 (paperback)

Library of Congress Cataloging-in-Publication Data
Turner, Chris (Chris K.)
   Taking responsibility for learning and teaching : from principles to practice / Chris Turner.
       p. cm.
   Summary: "Although this book draws on theoretical principles and research, it is a practical guide to leading the learning in schools"-- Provided by publisher.
   Includes bibliographical references and index.
   ISBN 978-1-85539-785-9 (pbk.)
   1. Teaching--Great Britain.   2. Professional learning communities--Great Britain.   3. Educational leadership--Great Britain.
   I. Title.
   LB1025.3.T84   2012
   371.2'011--dc23
2011020722

Typeset by Fakenham Prepress Solutions, Fakenham, Norfolk NR21 8NN
Printed and bound in India

Contents

Acknowledgements

I wish to express my heartfelt thanks to all those who helped in the compilation of the material for this book, especially to the staff in the primary and secondary schools that were visited in England and Wales and gave of their time to allow me to interview them about their work. To my colleagues in the Swansea School of Education, Swansea Metropolitan University, for their support and encouragement. Finally, to the staff at Continuum for their advice and guidance.

This book is dedicated to my family, especially to my sons Ben, Sam and Jack.

Part 1
Principles

1 Introduction

Background and Rationale

At first sight, taking responsibility for learning and teaching may seem to be an odd choice of title, but it reflects the reality in classrooms in schools in England and Wales. More traditional approaches to pedagogy have tended to place the onus on the teacher alone for standards of teaching and learning. For example, Gleeson and Gunter (2001) discussed the rationale for teacher accountability in the context of the introduction of performance management. Whilst the classroom teacher retains this responsibility, pupils themselves are now being encouraged to take more ownership and responsibility for their own learning. This is the case in schools in both countries, even allowing for differences in emphasis in education policy. This idea of ownership and control over what might be learned and how some pupils might learn extends to the work of support staff, who play a key role, usually in the form of targeted interventions. Clearly, SEN (Special Educational Needs) pupils require some support on their learning journey, although the deployment of TAs (teaching assistants) requires very careful consideration following the recent publication of research indicating they can have a negative impact on pupils' academic progress (Webster et al., 2011).

At the outset, it is necessary to spell out the main purposes of this book. These are to:

- provide an opportunity for practitioners to have a '**voice**', which may illuminate how they work with pupils in the classroom to enhance learning;
- enable practitioners to explain how they work with their **colleagues** to influence directly or indirectly the quality of teaching and learning in the school;
- outline some of the **similarities** and some of the **differences between teachers working in primary and secondary schools in England and Wales**, with reference to their approaches to pupils' learning.

The first two purposes outlined above can be considered as being the teacher 'leading the learning' with the pupils he or she teaches and that teacher extending his or her sphere of influence as a leader by the work done with colleagues, i.e. other teachers and support staff. The phrase 'leading the learning' is one which is in vogue at the present time. However, it can easily be represented as 'a good thing' in an uncritical way. This is because the phrase is laden with assumptions and is easily capable of being misinterpreted. Why might any consideration of leading the learning be important? One reason would be the desire to see standards of teaching and learning improve and thus contribute to school improvement, a 'bottom-up' philosophy that runs counter to so much 'top-down' change in the form of government-inspired target-driven initiatives, which are often short-term quick fixes to produce desirable outcomes. Such a philosophy requires a significant shift in policy and the present government's recently published white paper on education (DfE, 2010) may represent the first steps in recognizing the importance of the quality of classroom teachers.

At its most fundamental level, school improvement will not occur unless attempts to bring about desirable outcomes in terms of pupil learning are focused at the classroom level. In other words, the teacher's ability to effectively 'lead the learning' is fundamental in improving standards of pupils' attainment (Durrant and Holden, 2006; Harris and Muijs, 2005; Lingard et al., 2003). This implies that teachers can directly influence what is learned (whether it be knowledge, understanding or skills), how it is learned *and* why it is worth learning.

The four main assumptions made by the author in this book that underpin the concept of 'leading the learning' are:

- **Teachers as leaders of learning**
  Any teacher regardless of the length of time spent in the classroom will exercise leadership depending on the specific context (i.e. with pupils and possibly with other staff) in which that teacher is operating.

- **Collaboration as a choice**
  It is possible for all teachers to lead the learning in the fullest sense of that idea, but not all teachers wish to do so. They may choose not to collaborate with their colleagues to any great extent or even feel that there is anyone else with whom they can work closely.

- **Teachers are influential in the learning process – pupils are influential as well**
  The concept of leadership is conceptualized as a form of influence on pupils' learning in the classroom. In addition to developing pupils' cognitive abilities, such influence as the teacher exerts might also involve: social aspects (e.g. relating to behaviour); moral and spiritual aspects (e.g. living out desirable values by modelling them in the classroom); political considerations (e.g. modelling how to negotiate with pupils); and cultural concerns (e.g. explaining why some things are worth learning). Teachers can influence the attitudes of other staff to classroom pedagogy in formal meetings and informal discussions.

  In conjunction with this, it is also assumed that pupils can influence the teacher in relation to the direction of the learning process; i.e. influence is reciprocal. The teacher can quickly establish what the pupils might be interested in at any time (e.g. the Olympics) and exploit that context as a learning opportunity.

- **Teachers make a positive contribution to school improvement**
  Leading the learning effectively presents teachers with the opportunity, directly (with pupils in the classroom) or indirectly (when collaborating with other staff), to have a positive impact on the quality of pupils' learning in the medium and longer term (Durrant and Holden, 2006). Sustainable school improvement is *not* conceived here as being a short-term 'fix'.

Teacher-leaders

Throughout this book, the term 'teacher' is used to refer to all classroom practitioners, but not all teachers strongly influence their colleagues in terms of their attitudes to pedagogy. This could be due to inexperience or a lack of competence, which in turn generates a lack of credibility. Similarly, not all teachers manage to attain high standards of teaching and learning with the pupils they teach. Therefore the term '**teacher-leaders**' has been used to denote those teachers who are influential amongst their colleagues and achieve high standards because they are effective classroom practitioners. A given teacher-leader *may or may not* hold a formally designated post of responsibility in the school.

Teacher-leaders engage in an ongoing debate with their colleagues in school centred around the sharing of values and constructing ideas about effective learning. The backdrop to such a debate as this is characterized by complexity and paradox (Close and Raynor, 2010). There are tensions that arise because of the expectations of different stakeholders who each approach education from their own perspectives. The debate about what is to be learned and how it might be learned often means that teachers have to work hard to overcome barriers caused by low expectations; for example, persuading pupils that they can do something when they think they are not able to do it or encouraging particular pupils to apply for higher education when no one in their immediate family has experienced that level of study in the past.

An interesting conceptualization of a teacher-leader comes with the TDA's (Training and Development Agency) description of post-threshold teachers, who could be regarded as acting as teacher-leaders as they:

> act as role models for teaching and learning, make a distinctive contribution to raising standards across the school, continue to develop their expertise post threshold and provide regular coaching and mentoring to less experienced teachers. (TDA, 2007, p.4)

The main conceptual model used in this book is teacher leadership (Harris and Muijs, 2005). This is envisaged as consisting of two interlinked yet distinctive strands: firstly, the teacher being a leader in the sense of a conductor orchestrating the learning of the pupils and controlling their behaviour in a classroom context; and secondly, the teacher working closely with other colleagues (especially other teachers and learning support assistants) to share good practice, make a positive contribution to CPD (continuing professional development) and influence the direction of school improvement. The essence of teacher leadership is based on teachers' collaboration and co-operation with their colleagues to help them cope with an increasing set of demands made by successive governments, as well as recognizing their achievements in terms of classroom teaching and learning. This conceptualization of teacher leadership resonates with Gunter's (2005) ideas:

> educational leadership is concerned with productive social and socialising relationships where the approach is not so much about controlling relationships through team processes but more about how the agent is connected with others in their own and other's learning. Hence it is inclusive of all and integrated into teaching and learning. While there are formal organisational leaders who have a role and a job description, they are not the only leaders. Students are leaders of their own and other's learning, teachers are leaders of learning both inside and outside the organisation. (p.6)

It is acknowledged that there are limitations to the practical application of teacher leadership. These could include a fear of 'treading on people's toes', as classroom teachers would be well aware of the delegated responsibilities of other members of staff and a reluctance on the part of senior managers to relinquish their more formal roles as line managers, which might result in a reduction in real terms of the power that classroom teachers can exercise. Teacher-leaders rely less on formally designated, hierarchically driven positions and more on informal influence using their interpersonal skills and knowledge in the work-related environment. In addition, teacher-leaders need to be very adaptable in a continually changing educational environment and become skilled at 'creating the optimum conditions for learning' (Durrant and Holden, 2006). Durrant and Holden argued that this can only happen in 'a culture of reflective practice, criticality, professional dialogue and a commitment to shared decision-making involving all members of the school community' (p.154). This involves plenty of opportunity for debate, conflict and negotiation, thus giving an opportunity for the political dimension of teacher leadership to be discussed.

At this point, the reader may be wondering why any consideration of the notion of teacher leadership is worth pursuing when all primary and secondary schools have staff with formally designated responsibilities for leading or co-ordinating specific activities? Why might it be considered to be desirable to promote the notion of teacher leadership when a separate pay spine exists for those deemed to be the 'leadership' group? All members of the Senior Leadership Team (SLT) would be expected to take responsibility for a significant aspect or aspects of whole school policy. Adopting a teacher leadership role may not be accompanied by remuneration of any kind, so can the idea of teacher leadership be taken seriously?

The answer to such questions can be linked to the notion that school improvement is the responsibility of all staff (teachers and support staff) working together in collaboration. O'Donoghue and Clarke (2010) argued that teacher leadership is inextricably linked to teachers' learning because of its ability to nurture professional learning communities. Such communities potentially involve all teachers. They do not work in isolation but endeavour to collaborate with others, particularly where there is a common interest (such as teaching a specific area of the curriculum). Exercising influence over colleagues is founded on establishing credibility with colleagues, trust, sharing of common values, and the informal authority that comes with experience acquired over time in different work contexts. Such collaboration with other staff might operate on different levels on a continuum ranging from superficial to in-depth. DuFour (2004) argued that professional learning communities place a great deal of emphasis on learning outcomes, which means that monitoring and tracking processes need to be used intelligently to give feedback to the teacher as to how individual pupils might progress in their learning. An example of this is Assessing Pupil Progress (DCSF, 2010), which provides a way for teachers to focus more specifically on areas of knowledge, understanding or skills that pupils in Key Stage 1, 2 or 3 might further develop.

The Structure of this Book

This book is set out in such a way as to lay out the key **principles** that underpin the analytical framework in Chapters 2–5 and the practice to which it will be applied in Chapters 7–10, through a process of reflection and analysis of empirical data collected specifically for the purposes of writing this book.

Chapter 2, 'Teacher Leadership', discusses more modern approaches to leadership that emphasize its distributed nature rather than a more traditional reliance on hierarchical features. There is then a more detailed discussion of teacher leadership, which is the model (despite its limitations) that is used in Chapters 7–10 to analyze the data collected when carrying out research for this book.

Chapter 3, 'Perspectives on Learning', includes some key ideas about learning and their implications for teacher-leaders from three different perspectives: (i) general ideas about learning; (ii) pupils' learning at the classroom level; and (iii) learning that can be applied to adults.

Chapter 4, 'Educational Policy relating to Schools in England and Wales', discusses the educational policies that have promoted a number of government-inspired initiatives in the last ten years. One complicating factor in this discussion is the fact that the complexion of the government changed in May 2010 with the election of a coalition. It is clear that national priorities have changed, particularly in relation to policies that were being developed in response to the commitments made in the Children's Plan (DCSF,

2007). Many of these are now defunct because of financial cutbacks; e.g. use of targeted interventions such as the 'Every Child a Writer' programme.

Chapter 5, 'School Improvement, School Culture and the Micro-Politics of Change', places ideas about teacher leadership within a discussion of school improvement. Such 'bottom-up' approaches to change focus on classroom practice and operate in social, cultural and political organizational contexts. To effect school improvement, changes must be made. These sometimes take the form of classroom teachers implementing government-funded educational initiatives. Such processes involve some degree of risk, may not produce the desired outcomes in terms of improving pupils' learning and may not be sustainable in the longer term.

Chapter 6, 'Background to the Research', outlines the empirical basis of the research in which practice is located. The reasons why a case study approach was chosen are described, details of the case study teachers and the contexts in which they work are included, and the advantages and disadvantages of using case study methods are discussed.

Chapters 7–10 include details of what the principles outlined in Chapters 2–5 actually mean in **practice** from data collected in schools. Chapters 7 and 8 discuss the results of the investigations in primary schools in England and Wales indicating how the case study teacher-leaders lead the learning with pupils in their classrooms

Chapter 9 and 10 follow a similar pattern, discussing the results for the investigations in secondary schools in England and Wales.

Finally, Chapter 11 summarizes the main findings from the work done with teacher-leaders, giving them a voice and highlighting their key role in taking responsibility for leading the learning.

Note

The reader should note that, following a national election in May 2010, a coalition government took office and published a white paper on education in November 2010 (DfE, 2010), which heralded a number of policy proposals, the most relevant of which to teacher leadership were: (i) developing the notion of professional learning communities by publishing 'families of schools' data, which could encourage different forms of collaboration between teachers working in similar schools in their local region; (ii) to establish a network of 'teaching schools', which can offer high-quality training to their own staff and offer coaching for leadership development to other schools.

The research data for this book was collected between May and July 2010 and therefore Chapters 7–10 do not make any direct reference to more recent changes in education practice resulting from policy initiatives introduced by the coalition government during 2011. In addition, due to government changes implemented while this book was being written, the author refers to certain state-funded bodies, such as the Department for Children, Schools and Families (DCSF), which no longer exist.

Self-study Questions

1 (i) To what extent do you agree with the argument that classroom teachers have a leadership role?

(ii) What reasons can you give for your opinions?

2 To be designated as a teacher-leader means that person would have attained high standards of teaching and learning and be regarded as influential among colleagues. To what extent is it necessary for that person to hold a formally designated post of responsibility and why?

3 (i) Do you think you influence some pupils you teach more than others, in relation to their learning?

(ii) Why might that be?

4 (i) What does the term 'professional learning community' mean to you?

(ii) To what extent do you think that your school is a professional learning community?

2 Teacher Leadership

Introduction

This chapter initially discusses the notion of leadership in terms of two important considerations: (i) the ways in which power may be exercised; and (ii) the manner in which it is enacted in the current educational context. It is worth reiterating that the major focus in this book is on the work of teachers-leaders who attempt to influence their colleagues effectively and also lead the learning in the classroom by working co-operatively with pupils.

This is followed by a detailed consideration of distributed leadership, which is an important general organizational framework. In the context of schools, this has been applied to the notion of teacher leadership – the key conceptual idea in this book. Despite the continued existence of hierarchical structures in schools, teacher leadership is worthy of receiving more attention from commentators and practitioners as a way of conceptualizing leadership as it is exercised in primary and secondary schools in the second decade of the 21st century. There are two reasons for this: (i) school improvement has to be first and foremost based on changes to classroom practice; and (ii) learning is a joint enterprise with involvement from pupils, teachers, support staff and parents and teacher leadership places a great deal of emphasis on collaboration and the sharing of good practice. However, teacher leadership should not be viewed as a panacea – it has its limitations.

This chapter will then include a critique of teacher leadership that will reflect these limitations. The role played by other partners (i.e. support teachers and parents) in helping pupils to improve the quality of their learning is considered briefly. The final section of this chapter deals with the perceived links between leadership and learning (i.e. the links between the next chapter and this one).

Leadership

All the available evidence from a wide variety of researchers both in the UK and other parts of the world indicates that leadership in and of itself is a very slippery and ambiguous concept. Just about the only thing that most commentators agree on is that it is some form of influence that 'flows' between two or more people. This opens up the possibility of influencing the actions of others, their attitudes and generating collaborative activity. O'Donoghue and Clarke (2010) noted two important aspects: (i) that leadership is always exercised in a given context in particular ways; and (ii) that leaders and 'followers' can have interchangeable roles. Terminology such as this is often confusing as it is very tempting to think that the pupils, for example, being less experienced, may be cast in the role of 'followers' and the teaching staff are the leaders. In practice, there are plenty of occasions when pupils can exercise leadership skills themselves (pupil leadership) quite effectively, in that they can take more ownership of their learning and determine how and what is actually learned. Individual pupils can direct the learning in group work without necessarily receiving any significant input from the teacher.

Leadership and the Exercise of Power

Accepting that leadership is concerned with influence inevitably raises questions about the exercise of power, which can be manifested as authority or influence. Hoyle (1986) explained the differences between these as the former being based on a formal role within the organization (i.e. school) that is delegated to an individual teacher, while the latter relies more on building good interpersonal relationships based on trust, acceptance and mutual respect. In reality, an individual teacher has little formal authority if not part of the SLT. That teacher cannot require things to be done (i.e. as a form of coercion), yet many individuals, especially those who have gained a lot of experience in teaching, usually attempt to cope with a range of delegated responsibilities. Hoyle further described the nature of the influence such an individual might have on an informal basis. This aspect is very important in schools as some day-to-day teacher–teacher interactions are enacted in informal settings (staff room, corridors, the car park, departmental workrooms) when teachers are not otherwise occupied in the classroom.

Bacharach (1988) argued that the degree of influence exerted by individual teachers may be based on a combination of four factors: (i) personality (which may be loosely interpreted as charisma); (ii) expertise, which is usually derived from subject knowledge or the lessons learned from experience in the classroom; (iii) access, where an individual teacher uses information that is not necessarily freely available to influence the attitudes and opinions of others; (iv) resources, for example, modelling the use of the interactive whiteboard (IWB) with other staff.

At this stage, it is worth asking two questions: 'What is being influenced?' and 'Who is being influenced?'

To some extent, practice (i.e. pedagogy), which might take the form of an individual member of staff trying an approach to the teaching of a particular topic as a result of conversations with another member of staff. Some teachers are more influential than others because they have built up a bank of trust and credibility ('a track record') in the school, so their opinions will count for a lot, as far as other, less-experienced staff are concerned. In schools, it is often difficult to determine the extent of one teacher's influence on other staff, simply because the influence is such that it flows between two or more people in ways that try to work towards a desirable outcome as a result of their mutual interactions through discussion and peer observation of classroom practice. The trend towards more teachers engaging in peer observation (for example, as a result of mentoring and coaching) and sharing good practice within the workplace (i.e. the school itself) is likely to mean that teachers' direct influence on other teachers' classroom practice will continue to grow.

Authority, Influence and Responsibility

The balance between authority, influence and delegated responsibilities is a fruitful one to explore as it provides an insight as to the processes that occur when teachers work with each other. For example, one teacher might have a number of delegated responsibilities yet fail to carry out these duties effectively and can become discredited in the eyes of the staff to some extent. Thus, any wider influence on teaching and learning is likely to be minimal. On the other hand, a relatively inexperienced (often quite young) member of staff who has few formally delegated responsibilities may be quite influential in particular contexts, where he or she possess specific expertise (e.g. in use of ICT, which may be perceived by other staff as being innovative).

Gunter (2005) added to this debate two other important concepts: 'legitimacy' and 'accountability'. Teacher-leaders may claim a degree of legitimacy that is based on their acknowledged expertise, status or job title (formalized role). If they do have a delegated positions of responsibility, then that means they can be held directly accountable, which is important when it comes to taking responsibility for pupils' standards of learning. Alongside that responsibility comes some control of the work itself because, as Gunter (2005) pointed out, 'having the autonomy to make decisions' (p.43) is one of the satisfying elements of a teacher's job.

Understanding the ways in which power is exercised within an organization like a school needs to go beyond the purely bureaucratic and encompass the 'interactive aspects' (Busher, 2006) if a more useful view of leadership is going to be established. This is because the pupils themselves can exert considerable influence as key stakeholders within the school.

In as much as teacher-leaders would seek to influence their colleagues within a shared culture, they would also attempt to influence the pupils they teach to embrace a positive attitude to their education and, ideally, take more ownership for their own learning.

Leadership, Culture and Cultural Diversity

The importance of a school's culture is characterized by quality of the interpersonal relationships between the staff, between the pupils and staff, and between the parents and the staff and is reflected in the ethos of the school. At its most fundamental level, it is based on a set of beliefs and values that are shared freely among all the people who work in the school. A healthy culture (Busher, 2006) is one that can enable leadership at all levels to be exercised effectively. Among other things, this would be reflected in:

- high levels of trust between staff;
- the existence of strong informal and formal professional networks in school, even though in larger primary schools and most secondary schools this is much more difficult to achieve between different sub-groups of teachers who work together closely (for example, with a specific year group in a primary school or in a subject department in a secondary school);
- collaboration between staff in seeking to solve problems together and find ways of improving the quality of their teaching;
- risk-taking, which might be openly encouraged by the headteacher and SLT. In such circumstances, teachers can develop their professional expertise and their self-confidence.

Southworth (2004) advocated the development of collaborative cultures in schools, which would be 'characterised by teacher interaction, professional discussion school-based professional development and joint work' (pp.128–9). He also commented on the contrast between 'cultural nutrients', which help teachers learn from each other through collaboration, particularly in relation to the introduction and implementation of innovations, and 'cultural toxins', which can cause enormous damage to interpersonal relationships as a result of micro-political issues arising from conflict between staff.

Close examination of the available literature reveals an absence of any sustained focus on the relationship between leadership and diversity at a time when there is increasing cultural diversity in schools in England and Wales, both in terms of pupils in school and adults who work in them as teachers or support staff. Teachers themselves can belong to different ethnic groups and this is also true for teaching assistants, who may have language expertise in an EAL (English as an Additional Language) pupil's mother tongue. There has been a relative lack of research in this area and a lack of voice given to minority ethnic leaders, according to Lumby and Coleman (2007). They argue that the values espoused in the leadership literature are usually based on Western culture and believe that there are differences in the values held by those who work in hierarchically structured organizations like schools, which can be latent, or be implicit or unspoken, as the relatively powerless may feel unable to challenge the views of the more powerful. This could lead to the assumption that there is a homogenization of perspectives without due recognition being paid to the differences between culturally based perspectives due to ethnicity or, to a lesser extent, gender.

Distributed Leadership

It should be acknowledged that distributed leadership as a concept is widely contested and there is no widely recognized definition that has won widespread acceptance. This is partly due to a lack of clarity of what is actually being distributed and partly due to the difficulty of separating the idea of distribution from delegation. Distributed leadership is different from delegated leadership as there are always a number of responsibilities that need to be formally delegated by the headteacher to individual staff. Formalized delegation therefore places an emphasis on responsibilities and tasks. Distributed leadership is also open to the accusation that it is undemocratic and Woods (2004) argued that the idea is only tolerated in that it can be useful in bringing about compliance to or acceptance of an over-arching set of shared values and aims.

Distributed leadership is based on a relatively straightforward premise: all those who work together (teachers, support staff and pupils) can exercise leadership and influence the decisions that are made. It is presented here as having the potential to be a viable alternative to the notion of the 'heroic' leader who takes on a struggling school as a newly appointed headteacher and turns it round by creating new, clearly articulated goals, generating higher expectations and transforming the school's culture, resulting in better student outcomes. Such a model focused on the efforts of one individual can only provide a partial explanation for such a transformation. It is worthy of note that MacBeath et al. (2007) concluded that it was necessary to take a broader view of leadership:

> A charismatic or heroic headteacher may in certain circumstances be needed but the risk is that the template for leadership can be drawn too narrowly and may in the longer term be counterproductive. (p.138)

Therefore the leadership 'template' can be re-cast to draw in potentially all classroom teachers, but more specifically teacher-leaders (along with support staff and pupils to a lesser extent), who can help to drive forward school improvement significantly by, for example, being involved in small-scale initiatives that may involve an element of risk-taking but offer the prospect of directly or indirectly improving the quality of pupils' learning.

Accepting that leadership is exerting influence on the attitudes and actions of others, then reciprocal influence is equally important as people influence each other. Gronn (2003) argued for the importance of synergy, i.e. achieving more collectively than one person could do alone. Therefore distributed leadership may be seen when individuals work together in terms of concerted actions, pooling their skills and expertise to achieve a desired outcome. Gronn (2003) noted the importance of intuitive working relationships between two or more individuals who work together very well. Working together can lead to a degree of synchronicity, i.e. the production of agreed targets and plans between teachers working with teaching assistants. This is what Gronn referred to as 'conjoint agency'.

One of the main characteristics of distributed leadership is that instead of one person being required to embody all the desirable knowledge, skills and characteristics of leadership, different individuals can make significant contributions, which amount to a collective form of leadership (Yukl, 2008). That said, it is recognized that some individuals will always be more influential than others due to experience, personal charisma and/or status within a school.

Harris (2003) summarized the positive aspects of distributed leadership. It:

- incorporates the activities of multiple groups;
- implies a social distribution of leadership with any group that collaborates;
- implies a sense of interdependency.

Thus, collaboration between staff generates the possibility of building leadership capacity whilst acknowledging that the Senior Leadership Team (SLT) in any school retains the overall responsibility for what actually happens in relation to teaching and learning.

One of the attractive features of distributed leadership is that more 'ownership' by the staff as a group could well mean a greater commitment to the notion of working in a successful organization, generating a feeling that 'we are all in this together'. Admittedly, this might be easier to achieve among staff in a primary school context in comparison with secondary schools, simply because primary schools are usually much smaller in size. Distributed leadership is referred to 'inclusive leadership' as an alternative label by Jones and Pound (2008) in Early Years (EY) settings. They argue that there is room for everyone – including children – to take on leadership roles. This is because younger children can be offered the chance to decide how they would like their learning to progress.

Advocates of distributed leadership such as Spillane (2005) have argued for an understanding of leadership practice (how and why people do things) rather than focusing on role, function and routine. He argued that leadership practice is a product of the interpersonal interactions between school leaders, followers and situations. It is the working context that tends to define leadership practice. Spillane also provided evidence to indicate how multiple independent tasks are critical to the performance of a 'leadership routine' over time. For example, a classroom teacher provides the headteacher with a sample of written work from every pupil in the class. The headteacher can then provide feedback to both the teacher and the pupils. Such leadership practice resides in the interactions between the headteacher, teacher and the pupils. Other advocates of distributed leadership, in an American context, argue for the benefits of distributed leadership in easing the pressure on principals, sharing out leadership roles and placing greater emphasis on teacher collaboration. According to O'Donoghue and Clarke (2010), 'Leadership can be practised by those who hold no formal administrative leadership position, such as classroom teachers' (p.64). If the notion of classroom teachers exercising leadership is accepted, given the problems associated with asymmetrical power relationships that exist in all schools, then its meaning can now be explored within a more specific framework: teacher leadership.

Teacher Leadership

Harris (2003) in her review of teacher leadership included the attempts made to construct a definition of teacher leadership, none of which were particularly successful in capturing the essence of what teacher leadership is. This is not surprising given the conceptual confusion over the term 'leadership', which has defied all attempts to define precisely what it actually is. However, perhaps the most useful definition of teacher-leaders and teacher leadership is the one from Katzenmeyer and Moller (2001):

> teachers who are leaders within and beyond the classroom identify with and contribute to a community of teacher learners and leaders and influence others towards improved educational practice. (p.17)

Teacher leadership, they argued, has three main facets: 'leadership of students or other teachers; leadership of operational tasks; leadership through decision-making or partnership' (cited in Harris [2003] p. 315).

Frost and Durrant (2003) argued that there are four reasons why a focus on teacher leadership could be beneficial:

- teacher-leaders can help to achieve more internal coherence and consistency and thus develop school effectiveness;
- they can help to bring about school improvement by engaging collaboratively with other staff and carry out different forms of action research as a way of researching their own practice;
- they can improve teacher morale, which places greater emphasis on teacher professionalism rather than relying on salary increases;
- teacher-leaders can allow more democracy, thus giving teachers more control over their own work as a way of counteracting criticisms of the 'command-and-control' approaches that have tended to be used by successive governments in the last 20 years.

However, it should be borne in mind that there are limits to these benefits. These arise for two reasons: firstly, some teachers have designated responsibilities for specific aspects of the work of the school (e.g. subject leader, Key Stage co-ordinator etc.), which means that teacher-leaders would need to negotiate and collaborate effectively with their colleagues; secondly, it also relies on the SLT being prepared to engage in power sharing so that teacher-leaders are able to take some degree of ownership of and actively engage in school improvement initiatives.

Day and Harris (2003) argued that there are four dimensions to teacher leadership:

- **brokering**, which means engaging in the process of interpreting school policy in the classroom context, both with pupils and other teachers;
- **participation**, which can be interpreted as developing ownership as a result of staff, pupils and parents being part of the decision-making process;
- **mediation**, which means teachers helping other staff by sharing resources, exchanging ideas etc.;
- **relational**, which arises as a result of forging close relationships with other staff based on trust and mutual empowerment.

As far as the relational dimension is concerned, a teacher-leader would act as a team leader, working closely with other teachers or support staff in a particular year group in a primary school or subject area in a secondary school. It would also imply that teachers and support staff would participate in decision-making processes from a collegial perspective. However, evidence from Harris and Muijs (2005) indicated that classroom teachers were rarely fully involved in making decisions but were part of the consultation process, led by the SLT. Harris and Muijs also found that teacher-leaders were strongly encouraged to 'take a lead on initiatives' by the SLT. Collegial practice is only likely to be successful if all the staff involved are committed to the process of school improvement. O'Neill (2003, p.226) noted that: 'This commitment requires team members to acknowledge and value differences of opinion and to recognise that consensus may not always be possible.'

Harris and Lambert (2003) identified four key areas of skill associated with teacher leadership:

- personal actions involving reflection and evaluation;
- professional skills and knowledge, which encompass communication and responsiveness;
- collaborative skills, including team building and decision-making;
- change agency, which incorporates professional development.

They pointed out that not all of these skills will be developed in the same ways in all teachers. However, they offer the opportunity for participation in decision-making and for staff to learn from each other.

In the current financially constrained climate, teacher leadership may offer some opportunities for teachers to focus more on developing their own leadership skills in school (e.g. mentoring or coaching less-experienced staff as a means of promoting staff development). It may also offer an opportunity for a school to 'grow' its own leaders of the future, as so much of what happens is based on collaborative approaches: for example, a less-experienced member of staff job shadowing a more experienced teacher.

Teacher leadership, then, is not only exemplified in the classroom but is evident in the ways in which the teacher-leader influences other staff with whom he or she works closely. This inevitably is the result of some form of collaboration.

Smeets and Ponte (2009) found from their research on teachers working in a special school in Holland that various interpretations of collaboration were evident. These lay on a continuum from very little, where a colleague could only be regarded as a source of information, to very intensive, where teachers worked together and took equal responsibility. The effectiveness of teacher-leadership appeared to rest on the quality of relationships that existed between individuals. Negotiation also appeared to be very important as that process focused on values, outlooks and strategies. One of the more interesting findings from this research is that the influence exerted by an individual is mediated through the group of teachers working together in the school.

A teacher-leader will work closely in secondary schools with colleagues in a given subject area and in primary schools with teachers who work in the same Key Stage or year group. This is the main location in which the team building skills referred to by Harris and Lambert (2003) will be in evidence.

The teacher-leader may hold a formally designated role of responsibility (e.g. head of a subject department, team leader for Key Stage 2), but teacher leadership also contains informal aspects (Frost and Durrant, 2003), which are more concerned with sharing expertise, bringing or generating new ideas, helping colleagues in their teaching and having a positive attitude to new initiatives.

According to Leithwood in Bennett et al. (2003), personality characteristics that are highly valued by teachers generally include unselfishness, humility and intelligence. Values that are considered to be important are commitment and strong beliefs in sound educational pedagogy. Other aspects of effective teacher leadership include leading by example, offering support to others and being visible around the school. The ability to work well with colleagues is considered to be very important, as is being good at solving problems.

Exercising Effective Teacher Leadership

Writing from an American perspective, Lingard et al. (2003) considered that effective teacher leadership is demonstrated when there is a commitment shown to 'provide quality education for all students, not those just in their own classrooms or even in their own school' (p.21). This reflects Lingard's view that teacher leadership should be conceptualized within wider professional networks that focus on sharing good practice, not only within a given school but across a range of schools, which might form a professional learning community. Teacher-leaders can have the quality of their classroom practice acknowledged by independent inspectors (Ofsted in England and Estyn in Wales) and through careful analysis of pupils' learning outcome data. They can also help to develop future leaders. Lingard et al. (2003) commented that 'when there is an abundance of such leadership, where it is dispersed, leadership can be seen a process of creating other leaders, rather than followers' (p.21).

Clearly, effective teacher-leaders need to have positive relationships with pupils. They would avoid attributing a lack of success to perceived deficits (e.g. being due to poor social background or unsupportive parents) on the part of pupils but instead try to find ways of motivating and teaching pupils, particularly if working in disadvantaged schools. Lingard et al. (2003) found that teacher-leaders in situations such as this showed acute awareness of social justice issues and they endeavoured to make explicit connections in their teaching to the world beyond the classroom.

Teacher-leaders operate in their own specific work context and Frost and Durrant (2003) outlined four whole school factors that they see as being vital if teacher-leaders are to be effective in their work. Firstly, **internal support from the headteacher** and other member of the SLT was deemed to be very important. It could be that teacher-leaders work hard to set things up in their school but receive little backing from the SLT, significantly reducing their effectiveness. Leithwood in Brundrett et al. (2003) echoed the importance of support from the principal. He argued that the principal can provide individual support to staff; help to build collaborative cultures; provide intellectual stimulation; and can model desirable qualities of professionalism. Secondly, **external support** from, for example, staff working a local university Department of Education, where value is placed on enquiry, reflection, scholarship and debate, could prove very useful. Such staff could act as consultants. Thirdly, Frost and Durrant (2003) felt that extending the discourse through **networking** could help to build a professional learning community. Collaborative networks can help enhance the agency of individuals. Fourthly, they considered that **prioritizing initiatives** would be helpful, although this would depend on the outcome of discussions between the teacher-leader and the SLT.

In a similar vein, Harris and Muijs (2005) noted, from the results of their research, the support factors in the whole school work context that enabled such an initiative to occur. These included moral support, trust, respect, shared values, daily focus on being a learning community, cross-subject teams set up to break down barriers and boundaries and good internal communication.

Although writing from the perspective of headteachers, Southworth (2004) argued for the use of three tactics by teacher-leaders to influence the quality of pupils' learning, namely: modelling (leading by example); monitoring (which has symbolic and practical value); and professional dialogue, which is focused on teaching and learning in a classroom context. It is the last of these tactics that is worthy of a little more consideration as it might be argued that ongoing professional dialogue is perhaps the single most important strategy that teacher-leaders can use with their colleagues.

Monitoring and modelling are important if the teacher-leader holds a formally designated role such as Key Stage 3 co-ordinator or team leader for Key Stage 1. Modelling could be leading by example, but it is more than just demonstrating what to do and how to do it. If it is successful in inspiring others, then it offers the opportunity to transform practice. Southworth (2004) argued that, in an atmosphere of acceptance and trust, the process of professional dialogue involves asking questions as well as answering them, clarifying anything that is not clear and actively engaging in the use of metacognitive strategies (i.e. what do you think and why do you think it?). He also advocated the importance of articulation – giving a chance for the individual teacher or support teacher to express an opinion. Southworth considered that this is a knowledge-generating process, which modifies or adds to teachers' professional craft knowledge. He also added an important rider to this by stating that what classroom teachers learn is very context-specific, i.e. what works with those pupils in that class in that particular school.

In the context of educating younger children, teacher leadership is a complex issue in the EY phase (in England) or Foundation Phase (in Wales), as multi-agency approaches can present their own problems (Jones and Pound, 2008). Collaboration is vital in EY work and establishing a team ethos becomes a high priority. The team leader could be someone in a formally designated position. Establishing a common purpose is of overriding importance. The team itself can comprise of adults from a wide diversity of backgrounds (i.e. teachers, unqualified assistants, practitioners holding NVQ2 and 3 in nursery nursing, volunteers etc.). The work of Whalley (2005) cited in Jones and Pound (2008) illustrates the various actions taken by individuals and also includes ideas about leadership strategies that relate to those actions. For example, if the teacher-leader uses effective pedagogic strategies, this can 'enable the child to make choices and decisions, with appropriate support' (p.20). At a whole school level, 'leaders want all staff to feel that they have the power to make decisions and lead in their own area' (p.20).

Teacher Leadership – A Critique

Any worthwhile model that is useful for analyzing the teacher's role in improving teaching and learning needs to reflect the tensions, paradoxes and debates (Close and Raynor, 2010) that characterize classroom practice and whole school perspectives.

Four questions can be considered that subject the notion of teacher leadership to some quite intensive critical scrutiny. These are: concerns about leadership generally and teacher leadership in particular; debates that question the extent to which power can be shared in schools; questions about whether it is realistic to perceive all teachers as leaders; and finally, debates that focus on the viability of teacher leadership in a school culture that is performance-dominated, hierarchically organized and dominated by 'asymmetrical power relationships' (Busher, 2006).

Question 1 Is teacher leadership worthy of serious consideration when most (if not all) of the tasks have already been formally delegated and designated staff are allocated additional salary increments for accepting teaching and learning responsibilities?

Schools can be viewed from a structural perspective as they all perpetuate some form of hierarchical structure. Fitzgerald and Gunter (2008) have questioned the assumptions that relate to division of labour and the ways in which leadership is constructed or interpreted. They argued rather provocatively that leadership exists to make the system work better and that it can be seen as being a management strategy rather than a radical alternative. In its most basic form: teacher-leaders monitor the work of other teachers and ensure that standards are being met.

Fitzgerald and Gunter considered that it is accountability that is the main government 'tool' that creates pressure on schools to conform to its policy agenda. They painted a stark picture in the sense that those exercising teacher leadership may 'occupy a rung on the organisational hierarchy' (p.334) and may take on additional tasks and responsibilities with no pay increase or time allowance. Clearly the number of TLR (Teaching and Learning Responsibility) posts would be limited in all schools, although more so in primary schools compared to secondary schools.

There are some commentators who think that a wholesale reliance on teacher leadership would be misguided, as there is a body of other evidence that indicates that it would be foolish to ignore the headteacher's or principal's role in turning round ineffective or failing schools. Sugrue (2009), for example, commented that with the ever-increasing demands being made on senior leaders in schools, the role of the headteacher or principal would be untenable without some sharing of leadership responsibilities. He thinks that some re-balancing is required, i.e. some delegation in return for more co-operation and collaboration.

If all the research focus is on the ways in which teacher leadership might be enacted through collaboration with staff and pupils, then there is a danger that the headteacher's worth, recognition and status becomes diminished. This is an understandable point of view and it is accepted that headteachers retain the ultimate responsibility for all that happens in their schools. However, the teacher-leader role and the headteacher role are complementary and reciprocal. Sugrue (2009) expressed his reservations about teacher leadership in the following way: 'Teacher leadership has the potential to exclude, to be clique-ish, to be defensive and pursue teachers' interests rather than those of learners' (p.365).

Question 2 To what extent can power be shared in schools?

Harris (2003) suggested that opposition to the idea of teacher leadership could arise because it could be perceived as a 'fantasy', as power is concentrated in hands of the SLT, so while teacher leadership might be an acceptable idea in theory, it might be inconceivable in practice. After all, why would any headteacher be willing to let go of the reins of power and why would those holding formally designated posts of responsibility allow anyone else to take the lead in any aspect of school improvement?

Writing from an American perspective, Chrispeels (2004) outlined six reasons why headteachers might find letting go of power and allowing other staff to take on a leadership role difficult:

- Headteachers must pay close attention to the demands of external stakeholders (e.g. central government, local authorities, governors, as well as manage the internal school environment effectively;
- Headteachers can get caught in the middle of a plethora of overlapping mandates (in American terms) or multiple policy initiatives (in UK terms);
- Teachers themselves may be resistant to adopting new more proactive roles in school. They may wish to preserve their professional autonomy and may find any attempt to change from their current practice unwelcome. This could be true for older, more experienced teachers whose conceptualizations of the teacher's role and the headteacher's role are already deeply ingrained;
- There could be uncertainty on the part of teachers about the best ways of achieving high standards in terms of pupils' learning. In addition, the teaching unions may resist attempts to share leadership as they may see this as a threat to existing roles and responsibilities;
- Headteachers might find it difficult when they hold meetings with local authority personnel. There is an institutionally embedded bias towards a 'command-and-control' mentality, which reinforces the notion of 'do as I say' rather than any kind of collective decision-making;
- Headteachers may not have the required intra or interpersonal skills to work effectively with multiple stakeholders.

It is acknowledged that there are some barriers to teacher leadership. Formal leadership roles and responsibilities exist within hierarchical structures, more so in secondary schools because they are generally larger organizations. Leadership is socially constructed and is 'played out' in terms of the relationships between various stakeholders.

Question 3 Is it realistic to perceive all teachers are potential leaders?

The answer to such questions is a qualified 'no' simply because not all teachers are motivated to want to exercise any leadership skills beyond their own classrooms, although they would inevitably lead the learning to a greater or lesser extent with their pupils. Harris and Muijs (2005) agreed with this view, arguing that some classroom teachers may not see themselves as leaders and perhaps lack the confidence to embrace fully teacher leadership.

Given that teacher leadership is first and foremost a form of social, moral, cultural and political influence enacted in a given work-based context, it remains a possibility that any teacher could exercise some influence on the attitudes of others, on decisions that are made, whether he or she is aware of it or not. For example, it may well be that in a meeting led by a designated member of staff with a TLR, that person may well end up influencing the actual classroom practice in discussions about pedagogy. However, this does not mean that other staff will not also exert some influence of the decisions that are made. Leadership can stem from positional status and personal credibility and since schools are characterized by asymmetrical power relationships (Busher, 2006) the exercise of power by the person holding the TLR may or may not be the most influential in relation to the 'flow' of influence between colleagues.

Question 4 How much authority can be relinquished by school leaders without compromising the need for accountability?

Schools are very outcomes orientated and depend for their very continued existence on meeting expected government targets – i.e. they are very performance driven. According to Harris (2003), opposition to teacher leadership could be due to it being a form of 'heresy' because so much of the research effort in recent times in relation to school leadership has concentrated on the role of the headteacher, given the prevailing culture of performance and accountability. It is much easier to operate systems of accountability when they are targeted at individuals, i.e. the headteacher upon whom ultimate responsibility rests. The pressures brought about by external accountability may restrict teacher leadership as this might be perceived as being too risky. Teachers themselves may feel there is too little time available to carry out what might be thought of as being extra work.

An alternative, perhaps more positive, view of conceptualizing teacher leadership is not that teachers become surrogate monitors of other teachers' work (as suggested by Fitzgerald and Gunter, 2008) but it is seen as a way of recognizing and even celebrating the work that teachers do together, in collaboration, when grappling with complex issues arising from the implementation of the government's education policy initiatives. Therefore any discussion about leadership being solely about leading the organization needs to be refocused to being more about leading the learning. In this sense, teacher leadership is about alternatives: rather than focusing on individuals, it is the notion of working together/collaborating in an active fashion that is important. There are strong links here to teachers' professional identities, which an individual is forced to confront when answering questions such as: Who am I? What am I doing? In whose interests am I working? Am I more of a learner rather than a teacher in this specific context? Many experienced teachers would acknowledge that pupils sometimes can demonstrate skills (especially in the area of ICT) that are superior to their own.

Other Useful Theoretical Interpretations of Leadership

Scrutiny of the wealth of literature available soon reveals that leadership can be interpreted from various perspectives. Each of these tends to focus on particular aspects of leadership. By analogy, a similar situation would arise if one were asked to scrutinize a three-dimensional sculpture from different directions. Certain features of the sculpture would stand out more noticeably when observed from one direction compared to other directions. Bush and Glover (2003) have discussed various perspectives on leadership and six of them have been selected for inclusion in Figure 2.1 as they are particularly relevant to teacher leadership in terms of improving pupils' learning.

Leadership Perspective	Meaning for Teacher-Leaders
Transformational	They can articulate and share a clear vision of an **innovation/change** worthy of consideration or a modification to existing practice, which, if successful, will gain commitment from others. With pupils, they can challenge their existing ideas and offer to guide them through various activities which will develop their skills or enhance their knowledge and understanding. The 'downside' of this is that gaining commitment might degenerate into direct control of others, in terms of their thoughts and actions.
Moral	This has a focus on **values and beliefs** and may be based on a set of personal values possibly associated with religious faith. They could also be professional values that teachers could model for pupils, for example being curious, demonstrating openness and honesty etc. Moral leadership can certainly provide schools with a clear sense of purpose.
Participative	This may be interpreted as encouragement to take part in **school decision-making processes**. It places great emphasis on collegial approaches, democratic principles and empowerment. However, there are limits to this involvement owing to the fact that all schools are hierarchically organized and it may depend on the nature of the decisions being made.
Interpersonal	They attempt to develop good working relationships with pupils and other teachers. Such interpersonal skills are instrumental in developing shared goals and a **team ethos** among staff within, for example, a subject department in secondary schools or a year group in primary schools.
Contingent	Generally reflects the view that teacher-leaders' actions are dependent on the **specific work contexts** in which they are operating.
Political	This is an often neglected area of leadership because it deals with sensitive issues such as conflict, negotiation and bargaining. Teacher-leaders would possess well-developed interpersonal skills to help them **negotiate** successfully with pupils in the classroom and defuse potential conflicts, as well as enthuse other to participate and collaborate in school improvement projects.

Fig. 2.1 Alternative perspectives on leadership and their applications to teacher leadership

Partners in Pupils' Learning

Teacher-leaders working with teaching assistants (TAs)

TAs work under the guidance of the classroom teacher. Teacher-leaders are more likely to know their TAs well in primary schools as they will work with pupils in a particular class or year group on a daily basis. This makes it easier to establish and maintain an effective, ongoing professional relationship. In secondary schools, TAs are often deployed to help particular pupils as they move from one lesson to another around the school. This reduces the 'contact' time between the teacher and TA for them to plan effectively. TAs are usually invited to staff meetings, training days and to have an input into individual education plan (IEP) review meetings. However, teachers generally receive little training in the most effective ways of managing TAs so that pupils get the maximum benefit in terms of their learning. However, Watkinson (2003) noted the benefits to classroom teachers when the partnership with TAs is working well as it helps to 'alleviate the workload and the stress'.

Blatchford et al. (2009) found evidence from their research that pupils who receive regular TA support in primary and secondary schools tend to 'miss out' on interactions with the mainstream teacher. They used this finding to suggest that it may explain why there is an absence of research evidence to show that TAs are an 'obvious benefit to academic progress'. More recently, Webster et al.'s (2011) research indicated that TAs have a negative impact of pupils' progress, as mentioned in Chapter 1.

Teacher-leaders working with parents

Parents play an important role in helping to shape a child's attitude to learning. Although the role of parents in their child's learning is not the main focus in this book, it is still necessary to point out that sustained school improvement, to some extent, relies on parental support and encouragement to complement all that is going on during time in school to help the child make progress with learning. However, parents are a very diverse group, just as children are. The sheer diversity among parents is seen even to the extent that some parents are extremely proactive in their child's education while others appear to be much more reticent. According to Hurley (2002) this could be due to their low self-esteem, memories of their own lack of success at school and even lack of skills. It could also be due to language-related problems or a perception among some parents that little learning of any real value can take place at home compared to school.

Regular communication between the parents and the school is vital for both partners to be effective in helping the child. Sometimes, schools recognize the need to hold special events (workshops) to inform parents of important changes in the ways their child will be educated. Schools will try and offer refreshments and arrange several alternative dates to encourage parents to attend.

With younger pupils in primary education, it would be quite understandable if some parents felt ill-equipped to help with homework, but in general, it is far more likely that the main focus will be working with the parents to help the child to improve his or her literacy skills (especially reading and spelling) and numeracy skills.

Pupil Leadership

It clearly makes no sense to discuss the concept of teacher leadership without devoting some comments to the notion of pupil leadership by thinking about pupils themselves exercising some influence on their own learning. Flutter and Ruddock (2004) have discussed, in some detail, the contribution to school improvement that pupils can make. The legitimacy of pupils' perspectives on their own learning should not be undervalued. Pupils can be active participants in their own learning and frequently engage in self-reflection as well as self-evaluation to help maintain progression. Pupils can act as peer tutors in lessons, can participate in peer assessment and provide plenty of oral and written feedback to classroom teachers. There is also one further important element here, which is allowing pupils to make **choices** concerning what they would like to learn about and how they might go about tackling problems or answering questions that they have helped to devise.

The Links Between Leadership and Learning

In order to bridge the content of this chapter and the next one, it is worthwhile to focus briefly on the relationship between leading and learning. Leadership assumes human agency. In this case, it means the capacity of teachers to affect the working context, their relationships with pupils, other teachers and parents, and the pupils' learning. The concept of agency here really means being able to make a difference. MacBeath and Dempster (2009) argued that shared leadership develops teacher capacity and increases motivation and commitment. This may well have a positive effect in terms of student learning.

There is now more emphasis placed on social, cultural, cognitive frameworks of understanding the processes of learning: for example, thinking about one's own thinking (metacogition); asking questions; testing ideas; taking more control of one's own learning; being equipped to know how to deal with difficulties (Swaffield and MacBeath, 2009). These ideas can be contrasted with more traditional ideas about learning associated with the transmission of knowledge from those who might be regarded as 'subject experts' to pupils in the classroom who may be regarded as 'novices'.

There is a symbiotic relationship between leading and learning in the sense that leaders can be learners if they engage in reflective, analytical and evaluative practice and vice versa. They are inextricably intertwined and appear to feed off each other. Leading and learning both involve reflection-in-action (Schon, 1983): i.e. when a given teaching strategy (Plan A) is not working well with pupils, teacher-leaders have to think on their feet and put Plan B into effect very quickly. Similarly, there is much to be gained from reflecting-on-action as a result of a conscious attempt to influence colleagues if a meeting fails to produce the intended outcomes. Indeed the very act of influencing colleagues (consciously or sub-consciously) may sometimes produce new learning, which might be associated with unintended outcomes.

Swaffield and MacBeath (2009) argued that problem-solving skills are prevalent in both leading and learning. To solve a problem requires a decision to be made and teacher-leaders may well play a significant part in that process. At the same time, new learning may result on the part of pupils when they are confronted with a problem that challenges their existing skills-set or level of understanding.

Consideration of such a close relationship between leading and learning led Southworth (2004) to suggest an additional perspective on leadership, which he called 'learner-centred leadership'. This he described as 'a process of influencing teacher colleagues to develop, refine, enhance and transform their teaching and pupils' learning in classrooms' (p.114). Such a perspective arose from a discussion about leading in primary schools and is worthy of mention here because of its similarity to teacher leadership. However, there are two main differences, which can be summarized as: (i) the assumption that it is mainly members of the SLT who influence teachers' attitudes and practice; and (ii) it downgrades the possibility of teachers influencing their colleagues outside the classroom.

Summary

Distributed leadership is an important concept because if it is ignored and all the emphasis is placed on the strategic leadership provided by SLTs as well as on those staff who have formally designated responsibilities, improvements in pupils' standards of learning will not be sustained and will certainly convey an impression among classroom teachers that they do not have any real ownership of the change process. However, this is not without its own problems, as it forces SLTs and governors to devolve some power to other staff whilst at the same time remaining publically accountable for learning outcomes to a wider public audience (i.e. parents, the local authority, employers etc.). Active involvement in change goes hand-in-hand with some element of risk-taking where the outcomes might not always be predictable, in terms of achieving a set of desired learning outcomes.

Teacher leadership is a useful model for classroom-based teacher-leaders who in reality take responsibility for teaching and learning and also play a vital role in influencing their colleagues, especially in relation to pedagogical approaches. Leading the learning in the classroom might mean monitoring progress, modelling desirable attitudes to learning and facilitating pupils' own ideas about how they wish to progress with their own learning. Teacher-leaders may or may not hold a designated role or have delegated responsibilities but would still rely heavily on whole school support from a member of the SLT.

Teacher leadership is not without its limitations because all teachers work in schools that are dominated by organizational hierarchy and internal bureaucracy. However, it offers some hope as a model for teachers to be able to build ideas about professional learning communities involving all stakeholders, especially pupils, other teachers and support staff.

Self-study Questions

1 To what extent is leadership distributed in your school?
2 In the context of decision-making in your school, to what extent are the opinions concerning teaching and learning issues of all the stakeholders in your school (pupils, parents and staff) canvassed on a regular basis?
3 To what extent do pupils you teach lead their own learning?
4 Teacher leadership is concerned with the influence that one teacher can have on other teachers and support staff. Consider those colleagues with whom you work closely in the context of teaching and learning.
   (i)   Which of your colleagues do you think you influence most strongly and why?
   (ii) Who do you think has influenced you the most strongly and why?
5 Following on from the critique offered in this chapter about teacher leadership, are there any other aspects that might be considered to be problematic, and if so, what might they be?
6 Re-examine Busher's (2006) description of a 'healthy' culture that has been included in this chapter. To what extent would you describe the culture in your school as healthy?
7 Teacher-leaders develop, mainly through experience, the ability to solve problems (Swaffield and MacBeath, 2009). Yet these skills are enacted in two different contexts, i.e. problem-solving in relation to classroom learning with pupils or dealing with specific issues with colleagues. What are the main similarities and differences the teacher-leader might encounter when engaged in problem-solving in these two contexts?

3 Perspectives on Learning

Introduction

This chapter is divided into three sections. The first deals with some general aspects of learning that apply to a greater or lesser degree to both pupils and adults (teachers and support staff). It includes some discussion of learning in relation to cognitive, social and emotional perspectives. The second section deals with learning from an adult perspective including the implications for teacher-leaders working with other staff. Here the topics include informal learning and learning from experience, professional knowledge development, and coaching and mentoring. The final section discusses some perspectives on learning that are directly relevant to pupils, particularly individual and collaborative models of learning in the classroom, understanding more about the conditions for effective pupils' learning and pupils learning to learn. Unfortunately, there is not enough space available to allow a more in-depth treatment of some of the issues concerned with learning that are dealt with in this chapter.

In addition to the general assumptions made in Chapter 1, there are two additional assumptions that are worthy of mention here. Firstly, teachers as well as pupils learn as they gain experience, but, inevitably, some teachers question, reflect on and evaluate these experiences in more depth than others. Perhaps this is one of the hallmarks of teacher-leaders in that they can not only harness the significant aspects that have been learned but they can also articulate them well enough for their views to influence others in terms of their classroom practice. Secondly, all classroom teachers are primarily responsible for their own learning (which is self-directed) as well as shouldering the responsibility for pupils' learning.

Section 1 Some General Aspects of Learning

Shallow and Deep Learning

Loughran (2010) provided a useful discussion of the key differences between shallow and deep learning. He defined deep learning as 'examining new facts and ideas critically and tying them into existing cognitive structures and making numerous links between ideas' (p.30) and shallow (or surface) learning as 'accepting new facts and ideas uncritically and attempting to store them as isolated, unconnected items' (p.30).

Bowring-Carr and West-Burnham (1997) proposed a number of aspects to illustrate the differences between deep and shallow learning. **Learning as changing as a person**, they argued, is deep learning when previously held conceptions and perceptions are challenged and new ideas develop. Deep learning occurs when attempting to make sense of reality by carrying out some analysis or evaluation. On the other hand, **learning as memorization** can be categorized as shallow learning, as very little active thought is involved.

For teachers, shallow learning may be in evidence when a trainee teacher uses closed questions in a lesson in a very superficial fashion and gathers very little feedback from the pupils about their learning. By contrast, deep learning can occur when a teacher, having gained further experience, fully understands the principles that underpin assessment for learning (AfL) and can now translate them into classroom practice effectively (for example, use different questioning techniques with pupils; use peer and self-assessment procedures when appropriate etc.).

For pupils, shallow learning can be illustrated in terms of simple rules (e.g. for spelling or the order of numbers when counting), which then may assist the learner when tackling more challenging tasks. It involves little conscious thought and will decay from the working memory if not used frequently. Deep learning can be in evidence when attempting to understand abstract concepts or make connections between various ideas (for example, when thinking about why animals like polar bears are well suited to survive in the harsh arctic climate).

Loughran (2010) pointed out that it would be an error to consider that shallow learning is 'bad' and deep learning is 'good', as in some contexts learning may require a surface approach. However, an important metacognitive element may be involved, so, in the case of the trainee teacher mentioned earlier, questions such as 'How could I get more feedback from different pupils in the class?' and 'How can I use whole-class questioning sequences more effectively?' may generate deeper learning.

Those aspects of learning that apply to a greater or lesser degree to both teachers (including support staff) and pupils will now be discussed, in the context of the cognitive, social and emotional perspectives.

The Cognitive Dimension to Learning

Learning and the brain functions

Illeris (2007) claimed that the most significant recent discovery made in the field of brain research is the finding that reason and emotion cannot function independently of each other. Therefore, for a few individuals, while they may have the ability to use reason or their intelligence effectively, they cannot use either appropriately because of brain damage to the connections between the parts of the brain that control emotion and other parts that control reason. This is explained by the fact that the regulation produced by the emotions is not functioning. This is particularly applicable to problems that arise in decision-making and social interactions where behaviour might be considered to be unreasonable or inappropriate because the part of the brain controlling emotions is failing to control reasoning powers.

The mental functions controlled by the brain enable certain capabilities such as language, thought and self-identity to be developed in human beings. For example, thinking and communication skills develop, according to Illeris (2007), when there is a process of ongoing interaction between individuals and their environment, leading to new learning. This is an acquisition process that involves new content being learned coupled with the necessary motivation, will or desire to do it. Illeris developed a more complex model of learning, which he called the three dimensions of learning:

Content	Knowledge, understanding and skills to develop meaning (making sense of reality as it is perceived) (cognitive dimension);
Incentive	Human beings driven by internal needs (Maslow, 1954), extrinsic and intrinsic motivation, and affected by emotional responses;
Interaction	Essential part of human existence with the need to communicate (social dimension).

The content refers to learning new knowledge, understanding and skills; the incentive includes motivation, emotion and volition; and the interaction involves communication, action and co-operation. The content aspect leads to development of meaning for individuals and some insights into their own capabilities or abilities. The incentive dimension leads to the development (hopefully) of mental and bodily balance and the interaction element leads to integration socially, which is clearly very important.

Learning and memory

Memory consists of two major elements: short term and long term. The short-term memory has a limited capacity; the information stored decays rapidly and is heavily contextualized. The retrieval process from the short-term memory involves recall, recognition (often characterized by knowing the face but forgetting the name) and relearning (which is easer second time around). Learning begins with the individual detecting signals through the use of one or more of the senses. These are stored in the working memory (also known as the short-term memory).

The long-term memory has a very large capacity and the information stored there is permanent under normal circumstances. Information is stored in different parts of the brain – images in the right hemisphere and words as verbal symbols in the left hemisphere. Repetition and frequent revision is important to aid the process of information transfer from short-term to long-term memory.

The long-term memory can be further divided between the explicit and implicit memory. The implicit memory stores perceptual information as associations between stimulus and response mechanisms. The individual can then respond with his or her previously learned behaviour: this might involve physical skills (e.g. riding a bicycle) or priming, which means providing cues and clues. The explicit memory consists of two parts: firstly, the episodic memory, which links personal experiences to a time and a place, for example, knowing where you were at the dawn of the new millennium on 1 January 2000. Secondly, there is the semantic memory, which stores the meanings of concepts and our general knowledge.

Learning and thinking

Thinking is defined by Adey et al. (2001) as:

> Something we do when we try to solve problems; it involves processing the information that we have available to us – either from the external world or our own memories. Thinking allows us to take things we know or observe and turn them into new ways of understanding. (p.2)

Generally, thinking processes are regarded as an important precursor to learning. Thinking skills can be summarized, according to the DfES (2005), as information processing (e.g. finding things out); reasoning (e.g. giving opinions, making deductions); enquiry (e.g. asking questions); creativity (e.g. brainstorming, generating ideas, hypothesizing); and evaluation (e.g. developing criteria).There are many different perspectives on thinking that have been advocated by different researchers. Piaget (1950) perceived thinking as a developmental, active process with a focus on the individual. The Piagetian view was that learning lagged behind development; i.e. the appropriate cognitive structures needed to be in place. Vygotsky focused more on the social construction of knowledge in conjunction with other learners (i.e. learning taking place collectively in a social context). He felt that teachers should work with pupils in what he called the 'zone of proximal development' (Vygotsky, 1978). The teacher could then offer appropriate 'scaffolding' to enable pupils to progress with their learning.

Similarly, teacher-leaders may (e.g. through a process of peer observation) influence classroom practice with a colleague. This can be approached from a Vygotskian perspective (Vygotsky, 1978) in that they can traverse their own zone of proximal development (ZPD) when, instead of tackling a task alone (e.g. using assessment for learning ineffectively), 'scaffolding' is provided by a more experienced member of staff who might advise on the best course of action beforehand and give feedback afterwards. Such discussions can help to make more explicit forms of learning that otherwise might remain implicit (McGregor, 2007). To make what is implicit more explicit requires an understanding of metacognitive processes. Metacognition is 'thinking about one's own thinking'. Hacker (1998) argued that a person's metacognitive thoughts do not emerge as a result of interactions with external reality (i.e. the outside world) but instead, metacognitive thinking: *is tied to the mental representations of that reality, which can include what one knows about that internal representation, how it works and how one feels about it* (p. 3). Loughran (2010) felt that pupils can be encouraged to ask themselves a range of questions at each stage of completing a set task to encourage the development of their metacognitive abilities. This amounts to a process of self-reflection and self-regulation. He identified three broad stages: planning, monitoring and evaluation. One question at each stage, for example, could be as follows. Planning: What is the purpose of the task? Monitoring: How do I feel this is going? Evaluation: What would I do differently if I were to do the same task again?

The Social Dimension to Learning

An interesting conceptualization of learning, which can also be applied to pupils and adults, has been proposed by Wenger (1998). It is especially relevant to the work of teacher-leaders, as there is considerable emphasis placed on collaboration through social interaction. It is a more complex version of Vygotsky's ideas on social constructivism. Wenger referred to 'communities of practice', which are based on a social theory of learning. This has four elements: (i) meaning, which emerges from daily experience and is expressed through language; (ii) practice, which comes from actions and can result in learning; (iii) community, which assumes mutual engagement (i.e. participation) in some form of joint enterprise; (iv) identity, which is all about how learners perceive themselves. Wenger (1998) argued that each of these four elements change over time according to the type of trajectory the learner is following. He noted that: *a sense of trajectory gives us ways of sorting what matters and what does not, what contributes to our identity and what remains marginal* (p. 155). When applied to classrooms, some trajectories lead to full participation (some pupils become fully engaged with their learning), while other trajectories lead to peripheral participation. In this context, one community of practice would be pupils working in the classroom with a teacher and another community of practice might be the teacher-leader working with colleagues.

The Emotional Dimension to Learning

This can be a rather neglected area, which at the same time may have a major impact on the learning of pupils and their teachers. Harris (2007) has encapsulated the affective aspects (i.e. emotions and feelings) in the following way, to emphasize their importance:

> Schools are powerhouses of emotion as individuals engage with each other, with learning with their values and with everyday pleasures, excitements and joy that occur when relationships and learning combine in creative exploration and discovery. They are also minefields of disappointment, envy, fear, anguish, depression, humiliation, grief and guilt. (p.3)

For teacher-leaders, working with pupils and other colleagues in an open-hearted manner can be a risky business as self-esteem and self-confidence can easily be damaged, particularly if words or actions or both are misinterpreted. Building positive relationships with pupils and collegial relationships with colleagues can be problematic as there will always be the potential for making mistakes or getting things wrong. A willingness on the part of the teacher-leader to acknowledge mistakes is essential to maintain healthy relationships. Harris (2007) argued that effective leaders know their own limitations (i.e. their own strengths and weaknesses) and have developed a more balanced, wider whole school perspective ('helicoptering'), which helps them ride out the complexities and emotional tensions induced by the competing demands of different stakeholders (i.e. pupils, parents and other staff). The following comments apply to teacher-leaders equally well:

> Such leaders have an authority that is based on a deep understanding of self, a strong sense of identity, and a degree of self-acceptance which enables them to move beyond their own ego and take an aerial view of the school. (p.50)

Engaging with the learner 'voice' is a key element of teacher leadership. Many schools now realize just how important this is and use online surveys, asking pupils for regular feedback on their learning (i.e. what they enjoyed; what they found difficult to learn etc.), and relying on feedback from school council meetings. Such processes develop a sense of pupils' self-worth and the feeling that their views are being acted upon.

Section 2 Learning as an Adult: Implications for Teacher-leaders

Learning from Experience

This is perhaps the most important and powerful aspect of a teacher's learning. Kolb's (1984) notion of experiential learning is very useful. He defined learning as 'the process whereby knowledge is created through the transformation of experience' (p.38). This definition is underpinned by various assumptions, including the idea that knowledge is being continuously created and re-created or skills are being developed or refined. Given that a teacher's learning about teaching is heavily embedded in day-to-day classroom practice, it is appropriate to frame the next part of this discussion in terms of a simple model. One such is contained within the following framework:

Lesson Observation $\longrightarrow$ Reflection $\longrightarrow$ Analysis $\longrightarrow$ Evaluation

This can be thought of as a cyclical model in that classroom-based observation can be followed by reflection or thinking about the experiences, analyzing them and then evaluating their effectiveness. This is then followed by more observation, and so the process continues. This model will now be discussed in a little more detail.

Observation

The most powerful stimulus for teacher learning is classroom-based observation of the pupils themselves during lessons. This can be revealed by noting their degree of engagement, motivation, emotional responses, interpersonal interactions with others, their responses to questions and their own work, in whatever form that might be. This gives the teacher plenty of opportunities for reflection-in-action and reflection-on-action (Schon 1983). Learning journals are useful sources of information for recording and keeping track both of the pupils' learning and what teachers themselves are learning. Such documents could contain notes on what tasks pupils responded well to and any they found more challenging.

Reflection

This can take place in action or on action and is based on ideas first proposed by Schon (1983). Reflection-in- action tends to be used when there is an element of surprise, i.e. the unexpected happens and we search around to interrogate our thinking processes, which led us to a false conclusion. As teachers gain more experience, perhaps it is fairer to think of them dealing with variations in responses from pupils rather outright surprises, in the same way as tennis players respond during a game to the variations offered by the opponent (Schon, 1987). Teachers generally have plenty of opportunities to discuss issues and exchange ideas with each other. This means that they can experience some collective group-based cognitive development in discussions with each other.

Analysis

This involves investigating classroom practice and then subjecting the findings from that process to scrutiny and critical comment by means of comparisons with what is contained in the literature that reflects the current state of knowledge about the topic. This, for example, could be an investigation into the use made by teachers of different questioning techniques and their effectiveness from the pupils' perspective.

Evaluation

Clarifying what the goals are at the start of the teaching programme and making the learning outcomes clear means that the evaluation can then determine the extent to which those desirable goals have been achieved.

Teachers have many opportunities to develop their own understanding of teaching and learning processes, as well as learning from each other. However, if teachers question their own assumptions and personal theories about teaching and learning, then self-reflection and self-evaluation can offer the opportunity to become much more insightful about pupils' learning.

Such a process provides a way for teachers to learn more about managing behaviour, trying out new pedagogical techniques etc. Often very inexperienced teachers begin life in the classroom with some implicit (and misguided) ideas about pupils' learning, but as time goes on there is opportunity for teachers to gain a deeper understanding of the learning process in discussions with other staff based on experience and by thinking about ideas contained in professional literature.

Teachers, as adults, have the opportunity to learn in formal and informal ways. Turner (2006a) discussed how these ideas apply to the Early Professional Development (EPD) of inexperienced teachers, and a similar approach will be adopted here for teacher-leaders.

Formal learning

Eraut (2000) has proposed that formal learning can consist of a number of specific elements, e.g. the award of a qualification or participation in a prescribed event such as performance management. It can also mean attending courses run by a local authority or other outside agency, which may lead to some formal accreditation, for example, attending a course on health and safety, which then leads to a first-aid qualification. Figure 3.1 shows how the elements of formal learning might apply to teacher-leaders.

Structural Elements	Application to Teacher-Leaders
Prescribed learning framework	This might be partly related to the job description that accompanies a post of responsibility. It sets out the expectations the headteacher and governors have of the person and the tasks that are involved. In part, it might arise through the performance management process where one of the agreed targets may be related to involvement in a particular school initiative.
Organized learning event	Participation in an informal lesson observation of a colleague; giving feedback and engaging in a dialogue centred around sharing best practice.
Presence of a teacher	This could apply to a more experienced coach or mentor to whom the teacher-leader could turn to for advice, support etc.
Award of a qualification or recognition of achievement	The teacher-leader might be assessed and then be appointed as an Advanced Skills Teacher (AST).
Specific outcomes	Meeting the requirements to pass through 'threshold'.

Fig. 3.1 Ideas about formal learning as they might apply to teacher-leaders

Informal Learning

For teacher-leaders learning from past experience involves adopting selected elements of classroom practice of more experienced practitioners that are judged to be effective and have been learned by imitation and adaptation. There are also elements of learning that are intuitive (Claxton, 1997). Turner (2006b) suggested that 'intuitive thinking can govern actions without conscious thought' (p.424) and argued that informal learning can consist of three elements, based on the work of Eraut (2004). Eraut proposed that informal learning has three elements: (i) implicit learning, which is learning that takes place sub-consciously and is difficult to make explicit to others (Reber, 1993); (ii) reactive learning, which is based on immediate action with little or no time for any form of reflection and characterizes so much of what happens in a lesson when teachers have to make constant changes to their original intentions at the start of a lesson in the light of feedback from pupils about their difficulties; and (iii) deliberative learning, where definite learning goals are identified and time is set aside for discussion with the teacher-leader acting as a mentor or coach, which might, for example, involve discussing ways of improving the quality of formative assessment used by the colleague. All of this suggests that the full extent of the influence of a teacher-leader on colleagues would be very difficult to ascertain fully.

Learning and the Development of Professional Knowledge

The assumption made here is that an understanding of the work of teacher-leaders in helping to enhance teaching and learning may be illuminated by theoretical ideas about professional knowledge. This presupposes that teacher-leaders will conceptualize the role as a proactive one. Eraut (1994) argued for the existence of six categories of knowledge, i.e. knowledge of people, situational knowledge, knowledge of educational practice, conceptual knowledge, process knowledge and control knowledge. Turner (2006b) used these ideas when discussing the professional knowledge of subject leaders in secondary schools, but they can equally well be applied to teacher-leaders.

(i)   Knowledge of people: teacher-leaders would know their pupils well, in terms of their abilities, strengths and weaknesses. They would also have built a 'bank' of knowledge about their colleagues and would know whether they might wish to join in working on a collaborative project.

(ii) Situational knowledge: teacher-leaders would have a well-developed understanding of their own working context and could therefore take advantage of opportunities to share with colleagues when observing practice in the classroom. They would know how to use support teachers effectively if planning a specific intervention to help pupils.

(iii) Knowledge of educational practice: the teacher-leader would be acknowledged to be an expert in the teaching of a particular subject or have expertise gained through experience in dealing with a particular year group in primary school. Such knowledge would be invaluable when considering making curriculum changes.

(iv) Conceptual knowledge: relevant concepts that might be called upon to provide a teacher-leader with a framework for analysis and evaluation of practice might include assessment for learning, monitoring, differentiation etc. This kind of knowledge would prove useful in a mentoring or coaching role with less-experienced staff.

(v)   Process knowledge: this would include practical know-how in terms of monitoring the progress of pupils effectively in the classroom and also how to begin to deal with an educational government-inspired initiative when there is an absence of clear guidance (which is often the case!) and establish some sort of implementation plan.

(vi) Control knowledge: this is based on self-awareness. Teacher-leaders can identify their own strengths and weaknesses, both in terms of their classroom practice and being aware of where they can positively influence the practice of other staff, and where they would not be influential.

Teachers' Collaborative Learning

There are many different ways and contexts in which teachers can collaborate and O'Donoghue and Clarke (2010) refer to these as 'weaker' and 'stronger' approaches.

Weaker forms of collaboration can include anecdotal exchanges, casual conversations and fleeting corridor contacts, which generally only serve to maintain lines of communication or act as information exchange opportunities. Stronger forms of collaboration are more in-depth, purposeful and likely to have a significant impact of classroom practice in the longer term. O'Donoghue and Clarke (2010), citing the work of Little (1990), argued that:

> joint work such as mentoring, action research, peer coaching planning and mutual observation and feedback, she regards as powerful levers of interdependence, collective commitment, shared responsibility, review and critique. (p.90)

Coaching and Mentoring

Bowring-Carr and West-Burnham (1997) mounted a powerful argument against any national government dictating what counts as knowledge in relation to pedagogy in the classroom and instead advocated more power being delegated to individual, experienced teachers. This could mean placing less emphasis on so-called outside speakers/experts who are brought in to run in-service training days in school and relying more on teacher-leaders taking up a mentor-coach role in circumstances where the mentee may lack experience or have had some form of pedagogical 'deficit' identified as a result of the regular performance management appraisal process.

Pask and Joy (2007) proposed a useful working definition of mentoring: a 'mentor is a person who helps another to think things through' (p.8). They have also tried to distinguish mentoring from coaching, as they see a coach as 'a person who helps me to think through how to get from where I am to where I need or want to be' (p.11). This is seen as an active process linking thinking to action. An extremely important aspect of this is the idea that the person being mentored knows where he or she needs to be both with the quality of his or her teaching and its influence on pupils' learning. The mentor can give appropriate encouragement and support as well as suggest how the mentee might achieve goals in practice.

Pask and Joy (2007) argued against the mentor/coach being the line manager of colleagues. They did this on the grounds that the relationship should be based on trust and enacted in the absence of compliance and compulsion.

Section 3 Pupils' Learning: Implications for Teacher-leaders

Watkins (2005) has helpfully summarized three different conceptions of pupils' learning, which can act as a useful starting point. These are:

The transmission model

Learning is being taught, which assumes that pedagogy is based on a transmission of knowledge model. It tends to presume the teacher is acting as an expert, simply telling pupils what they should learn. The teacher dominates the discourse in the classroom. Good subject knowledge is expected, but the emotional and social aspects of learning are largely ignored. Effective teacher-leaders will recognize the limitations of this approach to teaching and learning as this is a broadly one-way model, making little or no real demand on the pupils. Thus their role is perceived to be passive rather than playing an active role in the learning process. It puts teachers in the 'box seat' in terms of controlling the learning process and, not surprisingly, there is a great deal of emphasis on pace, delivery and modelling unfamiliar procedures or skills. However, it is of interest to ask the question: Are there any circumstances when whole class, direct instruction methods of teaching would be justifiable? Muijs and Reynolds (2005) claimed, from their review of research evidence, that such circumstances do exist, citing examples such as teaching rules, procedures and basic skills to younger pupils (p.39).

The construction model

Learning is the individual pupil trying to make sense of experiences. The key assumption made here is that the learner tries to make sense by actively assimilating this new knowledge or understanding into what he or she already knows. This process of sense-making means that the individual has to engage in constructing this new understanding for him or herself, sometimes with help from others. Here the role of the teacher is seen more as a facilitator of learning and there is a greater emphasis laid on understanding. When discussing learning from a constructivist perspective, MacBeath in MacBeath and Dempster (2009) argued that such a focus may bring to light misconceptions as the pupil attempts to make sense of his or her experience in school. It might also be argued that there is some surprise on the part of teacher when it is realized that there may be little congruence between what the teacher is trying to teach and what the pupil actually perceives is happening.

The co-construction model

Learning is building knowledge through doing things with others. This is a process of co-construction that occurs in a social context. Watkins (2005) felt that this is based on the assumption that learners need to be involved in collaborative discussion and argument. This is a small-group perspective on learning. The teacher is less of an expert and more of a facilitator of learning as well as being a learner him or herself. O'Donoghue and Clarke (2010) argued for the importance of Vygotsky's idea about social constructivism, which, they maintained, 'occurs in a social context and is mediated by language' (p.74).

Another useful idea is that of scaffolding, where the teacher's main role is to facilitate pupils' learning by asking appropriately challenging questions, designing activities to move pupils learning forward and acting as a role model by demonstrating how actually to do something before the pupils try it for themselves.

Swaffield and MacBeath (2009) made some interesting comparisons between more traditional approaches to learning, which place great emphasis on the teacher's role, and more recent ways of thinking about learning, which accentuate pupils playing a far more active role in their learning.

As can be seen in Figure 3.2, in the more traditional conceptualizations of thinking about what goes on classrooms, the classroom was dominated by teacher-talk and reliance upon the transmission of knowledge into 'empty vessels' (i.e. pupils), who would then be expected to regurgitate much of what they had 'learned' in public examinations, relying almost solely on memorized information. Teachers now need to be skilled in posing interesting and relevant questions that allow pupils to think, as well as giving them the opportunity to raise their own questions as a starting point for new learning.

Traditional Approaches	Modern Approaches
Learning by rote Conducted by the teacher Transfer of information from those who know (teacher) to those who don't (pupils) Knowledge reproduced in tests Compliance	Learning as activity (for example, researching information on the Internet) Teachers and pupils can pose questions Testing ideas Thinking about what you think Making moral decisions Analyzing for understanding Debating

Fig. 3.2 A comparison of traditional and more modern approaches to learning

E-Learning

An interesting, constructivist approach is the opportunity afforded by virtual or e-learning. Here the working definition of e-learning is taken to be 'online access to learning resources, anywhere and anytime' (Holmes and Gardner, 2006, p.14). Many learners now have ready access to a vast range of resources online, which they can search for, reflect upon, analyze and evaluate. One of the problems associated with e-learning is the lack of face-to-face contact with another person or people to bounce ideas off and quickly to check out or even clarify meaning. This lack of opportunity means that there is less chance of the process of the social construction of knowledge (Vygotsky, 1978) taking place, i.e. making sense of reality by checking out what has been observed and understand with another (often more experienced) person in order to develop one's own understanding. Yet it is possible to set up online discussion groups for pupils and teachers, and this method would be favoured where the members of such a group are widely scattered geographically.

Teachers have always used a mixture of methods and technologies. Access to digital technologies has widened considerably in the last 20 years, both in schools and at home, mainly for reasons of affordability. Teachers can now take advantage of material available for pupils to use on the Internet and also set up their work space within virtual learning environments like Moodle.

The concept of 'blended learning' has been introduced to accommodate a mixture of virtual learning using distance-learning methods and face-to-face learning. Jordan et al. (2008) argued that blended learning represents a compromise, as using software for teaching purposes, without any involvement from a teacher, proved very expensive to develop. Blended learning can take many different forms depending on the context in which learning is taking place. Among the potential advantages mentioned by Jordan et al. (2008, pp.228–9) that are particularly relevant to work of teacher-leaders are:

Knowledge construction	Learners are actively engaged in the learning process as they interact with a range of materials and technologies;
Collaboration	Communication and collaboration with peers and teachers or experts enhance and develop learning and knowledge;
Interactivity	Learners interact with technology and are motivated to direct their own learning;
Reflection	E-mail, bulletin boards and blogs focus learners' attention and encourage them to reflect on what they write.

It is worth stating that not all pupils will be able to use online materials without some additional support. In addition, any kind of material represented visually is capable of being misinterpreted or misunderstood by pupils.

Another useful perspective, applicable to teachers and pupils, is communal learning via networks. This is underpinned by the notion of communal constructivism originally coined by Holmes et al. (2001). This may be defined as:

> an approach to learning in which students construct their own knowledge as a result of their experiences and interactions with others and are afforded the opportunity to contribute this knowledge to a communal knowledge base for the benefit of existing and new learners. (p.86)

Holmes and Gardner (2006) compare and contrast individual learning (by analogy with water flowing in a pipe) and communal learning (with reference to a river). The river analogy is more dynamic as it can flow over the 'flood plain' of collective knowledge year on year. There is likely to be more emphasis in the future on networking and team working as far as teachers' learning is concerned.

There are important differences between learning *from* others and learning *with* others. The former is focused on the learning of an individual and the latter has a more collective emphasis. Thus a group of teachers (from the same school or from different schools) can set up an online learning forum to share ideas that have been tried out in the classroom. An individual teacher can learn a great deal from online policy documentation that government agencies or local authority agents have published.

The distance-learning methods referred to earlier allow for two forms of response by the user

(i) Synchronous communication: e.g. video-conferencing, online chat facilities.

(ii) Asynchronous communication: e.g. e-mail; blogging; bulletin boards.

Both forms are helpful for learning from a constructivist perspective, but the latter form allows for more reflective comment to be made.

Pupils' Collaborative Learning

This assumes that pupils work in groups whose size varies according to the task in hand. Teachers have had to become more adept at managing small-group activities with pupils as there is now more emphasis on debate and discussion. Muijs and Reynolds (2005) argued that collaboration helped pupils develop better problem-solving skills, as some realize that other pupils may have devised better solutions than theirs. Muijs and Reynolds (2005) do not, however, see group work as a panacea. They identified several areas of difficulty for pupils such as: a lack of sharing skills, which can occur if one pupil dominates the discussion or tries to carry out what was supposed to be a group activity alone; a lack of participation skills because a given pupil lacks confidence; a lack of communication skills that may arise should a pupil have speech and language difficulties; a lack of listening skills where, for example, younger pupils might wait for their turn to speak without actually listening to other pupils' contributions.

Watkins et al. (2007) pointed out that co-operation and collaboration are closely linked activities. The former is possibly more orientated towards assisting an individual achieve personal goals whereas the latter is concerned with achieving the goals of the group. All forms of effective collaboration involve talk and the act of having to explain something to another pupil is helpful in clarifying and enriching meaning for the pupil. An excellent illustration of this was given by Watkins et al. (2007), referring to the statement made by Annie, a ten-year-old pupil in conversation with one of the co-authors:

You learn more [when working with others] because if you explain to people what to do, you say things you would not say to yourself, really. So you learn things that you wouldn't know if you were just doing it by yourself. (p.89)

Pupil learning takes place in a unique social context. The concept of sufficient challenge in the tasks tackled by pupils presents teachers with difficulties. Too much challenge will demotivate pupils; too little will not stretch the more able pupils. Responding to the challenges in learning in a positive fashion requires pupils have high levels of self-efficacy (Bandura, 1995). This is a very important concept, as pupils need to think: 'I can because I think I can.'

Ideally, pupils would learn how to be more independent, which might lead to self-regulated learning. They would engage in constructing new knowledge and under-standing through an active process of problem-solving and working in different contexts (e.g. outdoors). Pupils' prior knowledge is important, and this always needs to be clarified. New learning will only occur when it can be assimilated in what is already known (Ausubel, 1968). Over time there is more awareness among staff of the use made of particular learning strategies by pupils in given contexts.

Watkins et al. (2007) drew attention to the importance of interdependence when collaborating on a task. This is emphasized when paired work takes place in classroom through the use of 'talk partners' or 'think, pair, share' methods. These small-group techniques might also include the use of snowballing and jigsawing. Snowballing can be used to describe a technique where different groups in a class each make sugges-tions, which can then be debated with the whole class. An example of this might be a secondary school science teacher who is seeking ideas from a Key Stage 3 class that might explain the graphical results obtained when hot liquid candle wax cools in a test tube over time. The teacher would steer the discussion towards pupils' ideas to explain what the particles might be doing as the substance changes from a liquid to a solid. Interdependence can also be exemplified in the jigsaw approach to learning, where a given pupil acting as a temporary specialist on a given topic joins another small group to share what he or she has learned about the topic in a constructive fashion.

Conditions for Effective Pupil Learning

There appears to be general agreement that pupils learn in a variety of different ways. Dimmock (2000, pp.110–11) lists ten conditions for learning that make it more likely to happen:

(i)   A positive perception of self-concept and belief about personal abilities on the part of the student;

(ii) A motivation and interest to learn;

(iii) Goal direction and focus to what is to be achieved;

(iv) Meaningful connections between prior knowledge and meaningful information;

(v) Metacognition, where students are able to organize and structure their thoughts, as well as develop successful learning strategies as aids to understanding;

(vi) The state of readiness to learn, which is related to the student's stage of development and previous levels of learning; knowledge or skills to be learnt need to be within the student's capabilities;

(vii) Opportunities for appropriate practice or rehearsal; learning is generally enhanced by the learner practising the skill or applying the knowledge;

(viii) Opportunities for the transfer of learning to new or different situations, whether horizontally (across subject areas) or vertically (more difficult applications within the same area);

(ix) Appropriate amounts of reinforcement are provided; students differ in the amount of instructional help and time they need to learn;

(x) Appropriate amounts of positive feedback, realistic praise and encouragement received by the student; the family home and classroom environment may be relevant in determining how much feedback a student may need.

In addition to the 'meaningful connections' mentioned in (iv) above, Bowring-Carr and West-Burnham (1997) advocated the notion that deeper learning may be thought of as being the creation of personal meaning; i.e. this entails learning about the world and those who inhabit it from a very young age. This would include friends and family. It is reliant on trust and developing good interpersonal relationships. They also argued that learning must involve a constant creation and recreation of reality, particularly as pupils grow and develop.

One of the other conditions for learning in the Dimmock (2000) list is: (ii) 'motivation to learn', which includes the notion of challenge. According to Glover and Law (2002), the motivating force to learn, for both pupils and teachers, is determined by the need to challenge or respond to a challenge. A positive challenge is referred to by Hay McBer (2000) as 'a task perceived as involving a reasonable demand of knowledge, skill and effort' (p.36) and this is contrasted with a stress-inducing task, which could make (in the eyes of the pupil) impossible demands. This is linked to the level of expectations that teachers have of pupils, pupils have of teachers, and teachers and pupils have of themselves. Differentiation is of vital importance to teachers, to meet the needs of the pupils. Such a perspective fits in the personalized learning agenda, whose sole aim is to help pupils progress.

The importance of goal-directed learning cannot be understated. Goals or targets should be set for pupils' learning that ought to be achievable but challenging and should be accompanied by regular feedback on performance. Dimmock (2000) considers that target setting provides 'purpose, direction, commitment and, when feedback is given, reinforcement, encouragement and a sense of accomplishment, for students and teachers' (p.112).

One of the important elements of pupils' learning is the promotion of self-regulated learning. This is the idea that pupils can gradually become more willing and able to assume responsibility for controlling and directing their own learning. It is to some extent linked to Bandura's (1995) ideas about self-efficacy mentioned earlier in this chapter.

An attempt has been made in the Welsh Skills Framework document (DCELLS, 2008b) to encourage self-regulated learning by including the idea of success criteria, which should be discussed and drawn up by the teacher in conjunction with the pupils so that they can monitor and assess their own performance more easily. However, it should be noted that some pupils are not able, for one reason or another, to exercise this form of control over their own learning and it may remain as an aspiration rather than being realistic in the short term for these pupils. Most forms of learning are problematic (for example, some pupils have very poor memory retention) and also it can take time to grapple with more difficult ideas/concepts/techniques, which may be very confusing at first sight. This means that there is an element of perseverance necessary in learning if any kind of mastery is to be attained.

Pupils' Learning to Learn

There is a growing trend in schools today for teachers to focus more on the learning process and how children learn. There is more awareness that time is needed for pupils to reflect on their own learning process and its effectiveness. Making sense of learning can be strongly encouraged by giving the pupils opportunities to self- and peer-reflect. This can help to develop pupils' metacognitive abilities. Much of this process is supported by in-depth questioning from the teachers, which helps to make things clearer to pupils. Watkins et al. (2007, p.124) argued that helping learners requires teachers to:

- Help them to gain an understanding of their own learning;
- Help them develop the skills of monitoring and reviewing their learning paying attention to the goals and the understanding of their own processes;
- Maintain the message that a diversity of practice can be effective for learning.

Watkins et al. (2007, citing the work of Thomas, 2003) advocated that pupils are asked by the teacher to discuss with each other how they think they learn, to explain how they may have solved a problem and to think about their difficulties in learning. This process can be enacted in different contexts and is a strongly metacognitive process.

'Building Learning Power' (Claxton, 2002) is one approach to encourage pupils to learn more about their own learning processes. It consists of four elements: resilience, resourcefulness, reflectiveness and reciprocity. Each of these will now be briefly discussed.

Reflectiveness

Claxton in Atkinson and Claxton (2000) argued strongly that the capability to be creative and engage in problem-solving can only be exercised more effectively when the mind is more relaxed and stress-free (i.e. less pre-occupied). It requires time to 'mull things over' to allow possible solutions to incubate. Thus pupils need time 'to have a conversation with themselves', in Claxton's view.

Resilience

Pupils need to be able to deal with distractions that occur in the classroom and in the home environment. This is what Claxton refers to as 'noticing out of the corner of your eye' and can be linked to perseverance, which pupils need to learn when dealing with difficult aspects of learning.

Resourcefulness

This quality stems from an innate desire to be creative and imaginative, which some pupils possess in abundance. It is linked to curiosity and is therefore manifest by asking and responding to questions.

Reciprocity

The main quality being developed here is interdependence. Pupils can be exposed to a whole variety of different viewpoints by consideration of life in other cultures, when the judicious use of ICT can be a powerful learning tool. Teacher-leaders can model a degree of empathy for the attitudes and viewpoints of others, and pupils themselves, according to Claxton, can learn a great deal by observing other people's learning habits.

Summary

The overarching mode of learning proposed in this chapter for both teachers and pupils is a combination of individual learning (in terms of thinking processes, memory etc.) and, more significantly, taking responsibility for learning and collaborative learning. Teacher-leaders can collaborate with pupils in their classrooms and with their colleagues (other teachers and support staff).

Learning consists of three broad interlinked elements: cognitive, social and emotional, which have been illustrated in the model proposed by Illeris (2007). Memory plays a crucial role in learning, coupled with a temporal element. Pupils' thinking skills are enhanced if attention is given to developing their metacognitive abilities, even though this can be quite time consuming. If the processes of self-reflection and self-evaluation are encouraged, then pupils will understand more about learning how to learn.

Effective teacher-leaders work with pupils in their ZPD and set plenty of appropriately challenging tasks to help them move their learning forward.

Teacher-leaders learn from their own and others' experience and develop their professional knowledge in formal and informal settings. Acting as a coach or mentor can be a very effective way of influencing the practice of less-experienced staff. E-learning offers both staff and pupils extended learning opportunities, especially outside school hours and in holiday periods.

Self-study Questions

1 To what extent do you consider that there is an appropriate balance between the pupils you teach engaging in 'shallow' and 'deep' learning?

2 Given that there are three broad stages to doing any classroom-based task (planning, monitoring and evaluating), to what extent do you think you are developing the metacognitive abilities in the pupils you teach and when might those opportunities arise?

3 In what ways do you think your school could improve in terms of listening to 'pupil' voice? You could also respond to this question in a different way if you wish to consider 'learner' voice.

4 List all the contexts in which you have recently collaborated with other staff (teachers and support staff).

   (i)   In which context has this collaboration proved to be the most effective and why?

   (ii) In which context has this collaboration proved to be the least effective and why?

5 It can be argued that teacher-leaders can influence classroom teaching and learning most effectively when they are acting as coaches or mentors to less-experienced members of staff. To what extent do you agree with this argument and why?

   (i)   In the modern educational context, what role do you think e-learning has for a busy classroom practitioner?

   (ii) How effectively is your school's virtual learning environment used by pupils, and which aspects can be improved?

   (iii) Are you part of an online forum for classroom teachers? If you are, in what ways do you find it useful to communicate with teachers in other schools?

4 Educational Policy Relating to Schools in England and Wales

Introduction

There is an overarching policy context in which the research conducted with teacher-leaders described later in Chapters 7 and 9 in England and Chapters 8 and 10 in Wales is set. Effective teachers will inevitably interpret their work in the light of current policy and practice in education. This is not easy to discuss, given the fact that different education systems, which are becoming more divergent over time, operate in England and Wales.

In the last decade, successive governments envisaged greater diversity among schools in England. This meant that more schools were to be encouraged to seek specialist, academy or trust status as a way of bringing about a change in the culture of schools in general. Already there is a comparatively large number of schools that are designated as specialist schools. Academies are state funded but are managed by independent sponsors. They are usually to be found in inner-city areas and face significant challenges in terms of raising standards. Trust schools usually involve working with other schools to deliver the 14–19 curriculum. They are also designated as foundation schools. They can form partnerships with other schools to share expertise and create multiple learning pathways.

The Principality (Wales) does have some autonomy in its own decision-making processes through the Welsh Assembly, whose elected members meet in Cardiff, but the purse strings are held by members of parliament in London. This means that there is some devolution of power through delegated budgets, but the room for manoeuvre is limited. How this will change following a referendum held in March 2011 is not clear. A clear majority voted in favour of allowing the Welsh Assembly government to have greater independence in deciding how its affairs should be conducted in areas like education. However, in policy terms there are some commonalities but in practical terms there are also some important differences in the ways in which schooling is structured in England and Wales. Primary schools in England and Wales are broadly similar from an organizational perspective.

In Wales, because it has a thinly spread population apart from two major cities located in South Wales, there is a relatively high proportion of small primary schools serving rural communities. Most secondary schools in Wales tend to cater for the 11–18 age range, although the number of 11–16 schools is rising because of the economic need to offer a suitably wide range of post-14 and post-16 courses in fewer, much larger, more economically viable FE colleges. Unlike in England, there are no specialist secondary schools, trust schools, free schools or academies in Wales. Most secondary schools in Wales are either 11–16 or 11–18 mixed comprehensives.

This chapter will first address some of the key issues that help to explain policy developments that are relevant to teacher leadership and will be discussed from a historical perspective. Broadly speaking, there are four common policy initiatives that may be applied equally to schooling in England and Wales: workforce remodelling; the Every Child Matters (ECM) agenda; tracking and assessing pupils' progress, which was a high priority for the previous government, as outlined in the Children's Plan (DCSF, 2007); and personalized learning. Finally, there will be some consideration of recent changes in the curriculum arrangements and system reform both in England and in Wales.

Background

Education policy in the last 20 years appears to have been driven by an underlying attitude among politicians that the prevailing state education system is unsatisfactory and their task is to not only diagnose what is inadequate but also to prescribe what is needed to produce more desirable outcomes using legislation. One of the reasons for this sense of dissatisfaction lies in employers telling successive governments that school leavers do not have the necessary skills to enable them to function effectively in the workplace. An example to illustrate this was noted in June 2010 when the *Leicester Mercury* reported that 'School leavers were not up to work.' It quoted the chairman of the local branch of the Confederation of British Industry as saying that 'people lack the ability to express themselves and do basic mathematics'. Gleeson and Keep (2004) argued that, behind comments such as these, there is an implicit assumption that the education system should be expected to:

> produce 'job ready' candidates equipped with a range of skills, attitudes, pre-dispositions, and prior learning experiences that will allow them to slot effortlessly into a range of individual work settings and organisational contexts. (p.54)

This, however, is likely to be unachievable. It is unrealistic to expect pupils to construct for themselves an in-depth knowledge and understanding of the workplace, which exists in many different forms in the UK. However, schools could always do more to inculcate responsible attitudes towards work and employment, particularly in terms of the expectations and aspirations of young people. It may be possible for school leavers to demonstrate more evidence of the highly prized transferable skills (such as problem solving) as well higher achievement levels in basic skills such as communication and numeracy, which employers value, as a result of curriculum changes, which are discussed later on in this chapter.

One of the consequences of this situation is a constant tinkering with education policy in order to produce the desired outcomes of politicians. It may reflect an ongoing lack of trust in teachers as professionals. Such policy initiatives can also be interpreted as a deliberate attempt by central government to try and solve some of the wider problems in society (for example, families affected by marital breakdown, alcohol and drug abuse) by placing on schools more obligations to produce model citizens of the 21st century. However, the implementation of education policy at the classroom level remains in the hands of the individual teacher. It is usually the case that policy interpretation is carried out at a whole school level in the first instance, but thereafter the classroom teacher is left to use professional judgement within a whole school policy framework created by the Senior Leadership Team (SLT) and school governors and clear lines of accountability as part of a quality assurance system. Non-statutory guidance, with regard to curriculum matters, is often published some time after the policy initiative has been introduced. It can take the form of examples of good practice, which teachers themselves have laboured to produce.

As was noted in Chapter 2, teacher leadership offers the opportunity to empower teachers and give them some due recognition of their professionalism. Placing more emphasis on the positive aspects of influencing the quality of pupils' learning and collaborating with colleagues in a constructive manner can act as a powerful antidote to the more 'corrosive' effects on teachers of the imposition of ill-thought-out policy initiatives, which may have two consequences: the first is to produce an 'inner conflict' for teachers between their own beliefs about the best ways of guiding pupils' learning and what they are being required to do as a result of government policy; the second is to damage morale and lower the self-esteem of teachers.

It is recognized that any education system paid for by taxpayers will need to have monitoring and accountability procedures. There is always going to be a balance between trusting teachers' professionalism and ensuring that the best possible education outcomes can be achieved. As a consequence, much of current practice in terms of teaching and learning is accompanied by the need for schools to be accountable. School inspection regimes exist to ensure that education policy is being implemented effectively and increasingly that pupils perform to expected national target levels in core subjects like English and maths. This focus on desirable outcomes has driven the target-setting agenda and has created a culture of progression in learning that can be remarkably intolerant of situations where pupils fail to perform to expectations. The

Children's Plan (DCSF, 2007) indicated the former government's desire that a range of interventions should take place in the event of such underperformance. Performance management was introduced in schools in England in 2000 and in schools in Wales in 2002. This offers the opportunity for teachers to demonstrate that they are meeting the high standards expected for teaching and learning in the classroom.

Workforce Re-Modelling

A number of concerns were being voiced about teachers' work around the beginning of the new millennium. The workload of teachers was generally agreed to be excessive and is probably still the major reason why some entrants to the profession quickly become disillusioned and resign. The new Labour government elected in 1997 made no secret of its desire to place education at the top of its reform agenda. The Prime Minister, Tony Blair, indicated that he wished to see a world-class education system being developed in the UK.

In the case of education, this translated into a rigorous focus on the standards of teaching and learning. After a considerable amount of discussion and consultation with teacher unions about workforce re-modelling, a set of proposals was finally agreed upon (with the notable exception of the NUT) that came to be known as the 'Workload Agreement' (DfES, 2003). This agreement aimed to recruit more support staff in work in various capacities. Some were to help out with teaching, for example cover supervisors and teaching assistants; some were to be employed as personal assistants to help out with the considerable administrative burden placed upon schools and headteachers in particular; and others (for example bursars) were used to deal with financial matters. The employment of more adults in schools to act as teaching assistants helped turn inclusion, as a key area of policy for the Labour government post-1997, into a more realistic practical proposition. SEN pupils in mainstream classes now had access to more one-to-one help.

One of the selling points from the government's point of view that was addressed in this agreement was an anticipated restoration of 'work–life balance', which the teacher unions had been concerned about for a number of years. Whether this has been achieved is open to debate. The agreement was implemented over a two-year period from September 2003 to allow for limits to be introduced on covering for absent colleagues, the introduction of guaranteed PPA (planning, preparation and assessment) time and new invigilation arrangements. However, as Wilkinson (2005) pointed out, this agreement 'challenges the entire basis of teacher professionalism' (p.436), as these new arrangements tend to blur the boundaries between what teachers do and what higher-level teaching assistants and cover supervisors do (Edmond and Price, 2009). When thinking about teachers collaborating with other staff within a model of teacher leadership, this would include teaching assistants and, in the case of very young pupils, nursery nurses.

Against this backdrop of workforce remodelling, which has seen a large increase in the number of teaching assistants being employed in schools, and the implementation of the Children's Act (DfES, 2004), which required children's support services to work together to support more vulnerable children, it is worth briefly discussing team leadership in a multi-agency context. This is of particular relevance to teachers working in primary schools, dealing with younger children. In Wales, this would be referred to as the Foundation Phase (for children aged from 3 to 7 years old), or in England, the Early Years Foundation for children aged between 3 and 5 years old and Key Stage 1 for children aged 5 to 7 years old. In the Foundation Phase or Early Years settings, working with outside agencies is a daily reality for many teachers. This particularly applies to the situation relevant to young, vulnerable SEN pupils who all require some form of additional support.

In the context of working with other adults who are support staff, the teacher may be considered to be acting as a team leader. When working with young children in the nursery or reception classes, one significant feature is the sheer number of adults involved (including teaching assistants, nursery nurses and trainee teachers). Co-ordinating the work of other adults in a busy classroom with young children is no easy task. Teamwork is essential if the core task of ensuring that pupils learn effectively is to be achieved. This can mean allowing the individual interests of adults to become of secondary importance to the primary task of educating children. Jones and Pound (2008) advocated the importance of being mutually accountable; i.e. each team member owes it to everyone else to be accountable for whatever he or she does.

When thinking about the education of vulnerable young children, there is a great deal of pressure from government agencies 'downwards' for professionals to share information. Jones and Pound (2008) pointed out that working in a multi-agency context is a very complex process and relies heavily on professionals (e.g. teachers, nurses, social workers) and others (e.g. voluntary workers) from very different backgrounds being willing to communicate effectively with each other. It can be very difficult for the needs of the child to be considered from a holistic viewpoint. Successful multi-agency work appears to involve a great deal of consultation, negotiation, conflict resolution, exchange of information and agreeing decision-making procedures. Two underlying aspects that are fundamental are trust and respect being exercised among all those who work together in the best interests of the child.

The 'Every Child Matters' Agenda

An important piece of legislation that became law in 2004 was the Children's Act (DfES, 2004). This gave some legislative teeth to what has become known as the 'Every

Child Matters' (ECM) agenda. This was drawn up after widespread consultation by the government in response to the horrific abuse and suffering of a young girl, Victoria Climbié, at the hands of her guardians. The inquiry set up to look into this matter in more depth found that there were major problems with the relevant children's support services, who all failed to co-ordinate their activities and share information. The Children's Act required these agencies to work more closely to try and prevent a re-occurrence of such a tragedy.

The ECM agenda coalesced around five themes: be healthy; stay safe; enjoy and achieve; make a positive contribution; and achieve economic wellbeing. Each of these can play a part in different learning contexts. Two examples are:

(i)   the Healthy Schools Initiative, which was a joint initiative between the Department of Health and the Department for Children, Schools and Families set up in 2007. One of its requirements was to ensure that all pupils get some physical education on a weekly basis, to contribute to a healthy lifestyle;

(ii) Education for Sustainable Development and Global Citizenship (ESDGC) in Wales or Global Dimension and Sustainable Development in England playing a part to 'making a positive contribution' a reality, in the sense that children can be educated to understand more about the relationship between contemporary lifestyle and its often-damaging impact on the environment. It is also intended to help pupils make decisions that will lead to a more sustainable use of resources in the future.

It was envisaged that the Healthy Schools programme would be instrumental in promoting the wellbeing of pupils. However, there was also concern, at government level, that the risks associated with taking pupils on school trips (not to mention dealing with the copious amounts of paperwork) were being perceived by teachers as outweighing any potential benefits pupils might gain; e.g. learning new skills or applying their knowledge in specific outdoor environments. There was some evidence of a reduction in the frequency of school trips as a result of these concerns.

As part of 'staying safe', schools needed to be proactive in helping to protect children from bullying, particularly cyber-bullying. Whilst the all the ECM themes are important for teachers, teacher-leaders might be expected to be particularly effective in helping children to be active learners, encouraging their full participation and ownership of all the activities carried out in the classroom and consequently achieving standards of learning commensurate with their abilities.

Tracking and Assessing Pupils' Progress

One of the tools that has been developed more recently is known as APP (Assessing Pupils' Progress) (DCSF, 2010), which was a part of the National Strategies in education devised by the previous government. This is used in primary and secondary schools to track progress in Key Stages 1, 2 and 3 in the Core subjects. If it is implemented effectively, it has the advantage of less use of tests (e.g. spelling tests, written exercises in mathematics) and more use of alternative strategies such as examining a portfolio of work put together by a pupil over a period of time, which would indicate current levels of spelling capability and talking to pupils about how they have tackled a problem (DCSF, 2010). There are focuses of assessment that are described within each level of attainment in each of the Core subjects. Another advantage of the APP approach is that more diverse forms of evidence are admissible for assessment purposes (e.g. photographs, presentations, video). Internal moderation is a key part of the process, with teachers being encouraged to meet up once a term to compare the progress of their pupils against national standards.

Although the use of the National Strategies has now ended, APP remains one way in which pupils' progress can be tracked, even though the coalition government has signalled that it does not consider its use to be prescriptive (DfE, 2010).

Personalized Learning (PL)

Personalized learning has been defined by Gilbert (DfES, 2007) as:

> taking a highly structured and responsive approach to each child's or young person's learning in order that all are able to progress, achieve and participate. It means strengthening the link between learning and teaching by engaging pupils, and their parents, as partners in learning. (p.6)

Such a definition is heavily dependent on the teacher knowing the pupils well. It does offer the teacher-leader an opportunity to influence practice with colleagues, especially in relation to the use of new pedagogical approaches, which the teacher-leader can advise colleagues about, or techniques that have tried out before and have been effective in improving pupils' learning. The phrase 'personalized learning' has been widely referred to in policy documentation in England in recent years, but less so in Wales, where the notion of the learner-centred curriculum has been utilized (DCELLS, 2008a). However, the sentiments behind the different terminology are very similar, as in both countries the emphasis is on *progression* in learning. It is also the case that teachers are expected to set *challenging* tasks appropriate to the ability of the individual pupil. Improving standards of attainment in relation to pupil learning also means that a great deal of attention is now paid to detailed target setting in terms of feedback to pupils as to how their work might improve and what they need to focus on to improve their work further.

PL has spawned a whole 'industry' dedicated to tracking and monitoring an individual pupil's progress by means of data, involving the classroom teacher, support staff, members of the SLT, local authority personnel etc. Such data enables comparisons to be made to ensure that progress is being made in line with national trends and expectations and schools can be compared to see if rates of progress in one school are broadly in line with progress made by pupils in another school, assuming the pupils are from similar socio-economic backgrounds.

Clearly, then, personalized learning is not envisaged as being based on drawing up 30 different lesson plans for individuals in a given class. As has already been mentioned, it is more about how to move pupils forward in their learning, in terms of improving their knowledge, understanding and skills. As a result of the funded proposals set out in the CP, schools in England were able to offer one-to-one tuition in English and maths through the 'Every Child a Writer', 'Every Child a Reader' and 'Every Child Counts' programmes, which were funded by the former government. These programmes formed an important part of the National Strategies aimed at improving the literacy and numeracy skills of pupils in Key Stages 1 and 2. For example, 'Every Child a Reader' targeted individual pupils with significant reading difficulties with a one-to-one Reading Recovery programme. The programmes were a practical outcome of the Children's Plan, which promised appropriate support for children who showed early signs of falling behind their peers in the form of additional funding.

System Reform in England

As briefly referred to earlier in this chapter, there is a range of different types of secondary school, including academies. Academies are publicly funded schools that operate outside the control of the local authority. They are able to set their own pay scales and conditions of service, change the length of the school day and length of terms as they see fit and have more freedom to deliver the curriculum as is deemed appropriate. The coalition government is very keen to increase the number of academies (DfE, 2010) which it sees as a way of driving change through school leaders and teachers collaborating with each other without interference from bureaucrats.

A new type of school known as a 'free school' has been promoted by the current Education Secretary Michael Gove. The inspiration for these schools has come from similar forms of schooling in the USA and Sweden. They offer an alternative to existing models of school organization as they can bypass a great deal of government bureaucracy if they receive approval from the Secretary of State to be established. They can be set up by parents, charities, teachers or other independent organizations. They are very similar to academies in that they are funded by the state whilst exercising a great deal of independence. The opening hours of the schools will be longer and teachers will be expected to be 'on call' for pupils (i.e. contactable by phone or e-mail) when the school itself might be closed.

It is highly likely that teachers would only become interested in helping establish free schools if: (i) they had become disillusioned with all the policy changes that have affected schools in the last 25 years; (ii) they could garner enough interest from parents to set up an attractive, viable alternative to the current local provision, especially perhaps to large secondary schools that had been created as a result of the amalgamation of several smaller schools that had existed previously; (iii) there was a real possibility of taking more control and exercising more autonomy with fewer constraints, as well as the opportunity to take on new roles and responsibilities. Relatively few free school proposals have received approval to the pre-opening stage (a total of nine to date), but there does seem to be some expectation that the numbers will rise in the future (DfE, 2011).

System Reform in Wales

In Wales, there has been a great deal of focus on school effectiveness in the context of system leadership. The importance of tri-level reform has been advocated strongly by Michael Fullan (2009). This involves changes at national, local authority and school level. Above all, it is relevant to teacher-leaders as it is about building capacity with the possibility of using them as mentors or coaches with less-experienced staff indirectly to help pupils achieve better learning outcomes.

There is also an emphasis on schools working together in networks to help drive improvements. In terms of teacher leadership, there is an interesting statement in the School Effectiveness Framework (SEF) (DCELLS, 2008d) document:

> Leadership in the classroom requires practitioners to lead the implementation of pedagogy, curriculum innovation and knowledge about learning for children and young people. Equally it requires teachers to lead classroom assistants and work with professionals from other services to ensure children have access to appropriate support for their well-being and best possible learning opportunities. (p.13)

Such statements reflect the ideal scenario for teacher-leaders in the classroom context. Building collaborative cultures in school can help to build capacity for continuous improvement and embed the notion of building professional learning communities. The SEF document advocates the idea of building strong learning communities within each school and between schools. It promotes the notion of 'families' of schools, based on factors such as size and the numbers of pupils receiving free school meals. However, geographical location is very important in a country like Wales where the population is spread out over a wide area. Frequent face-to-face contact between staff from different schools in the same family that are located close to each other is relatively easy to arrange. Regular face-to-face contact between staff working in schools in the same family, but located in North and South Wales, is far less likely because of the distances and travelling difficulties involved. The possible sharing of good practice between staff is seen as one way to reduce variations in performance between schools. There is a wealth of data available that can be used to make raw comparisons between pupils' achievements in Key Stage 2, 3 or 4 within a family of schools.

There is an ongoing demand for school improvement and accountability within the SEF framework. The framework outlines the role of associates (working with between four and ten schools) who act as supervisors or even enforcers of this initiative. Such associates tend to be experienced and successful headteachers. There are similar arrangements in place in England, where school improvement processes can be assisted by School Improvement Partners (SIPs).

Curriculum Changes in England and Wales

The Rose review (DCSF, 2009) of the primary curriculum in England made a series of recommendations for change following wide-ranging consultations with headteachers and local authority advisers. Among these was the recommendation that the primary curriculum be organized into six areas of learning. The review also indicated the added value that cross-curricular studies can contribute to children's education when considering topics such as citizenship, drama, health and wellbeing.

In Wales recent changes have seen the introduction of the Foundation Phase as it applies to children aged 3–7 years old (DCELLS, 2008c). This curriculum shares many of the same aspirations as the primary curriculum in England (e.g. to produce successful learners who enjoy learning, make progress and achieve) but places a greater emphasis on skills development than in England.

Seven areas of learning were included for the Foundation Phase in Wales, with the Welsh language being the additional area. One area of learning in England (Understanding Physical Development, Health and Wellbeing) has been divided to match the equivalent areas in Wales. Religious Education is a statutory part of the curriculum in both England and Wales. Figure 4.1 compares the areas of learning in England and Wales.

Areas of Learning (Wales)	Areas of Learning (England) Proposed by the Rose Review
*Personal and Social Development, Well Being and Skills	Understanding Health and Wellbeing
Mathematical Development	Mathematical Understanding
Welsh Language Development	No direct equivalent in England
Knowledge and Understanding of the World	Historical, Geographical and Social Understanding; Scientific and Technological Understanding
Physical Development	Understanding Physical Development
Creative Development	Understanding the Arts
Language, Literacy and Communication Skills	Understanding English, Communication and Languages

Fig. 4.1 Comparing areas of learning in the primary curriculum in schools in England and Wales (*includes emphasis on the use of the outdoor environment)

Following the election of the coalition government in May 2010 and subsequent vote in the House of Commons, it was decided that the new curriculum proposals based on the Rose review, due to be implemented in primary schools in September 2011, would *not* be implemented in England. The current coalition government appears to favour a more traditional emphasis on subject teaching in Key Stages 1 and 2.

The secondary sectors in England and Wales both include very similar lists of subjects to be studied, except that in Wales Welsh is a compulsory part of the curriculum and Citizenship is compulsory in England.

There are two other initiatives that are worthy of some attention in relation to recent curriculum developments in England. One is an attempt to introduce greater curriculum breadth in both England and Wales and the other is PLTS (Personal, Learning and Thinking Skills). The coalition government's white paper on education (DfE, 2010) foreshadowed the introduction of the English Baccalaureate (EB) for any student who secures GCSE grades A* to C in five subjects: English, m, the sciences, a modern or ancient foreign language, and a humanities subject such as history or geography. From an accountability perspective, this will now become a benchmark that is intended to replace the more traditional, less specified five GCSE passes at A* to C target for pupils. This has divided opinion, as its supporters claim that the EB demands more academic rigour, whilst its detractors argue that it does not take into account performance in subjects such as Music or RE as well as more vocationally orientated subjects.

There is a corresponding qualification in Wales known as the Welsh Baccalaureate

(WB), which has been more successful, with high levels of take-up in schools and FE colleges. At post-16 level, the WB can be taken by students alongside A level courses.

Personal, Learning and Thinking Skills (PLTS) (QCDA, 2009) focus on the development of skills in the learner (i.e. pupil) that can occur both in school and in other locations. These are deemed to be skills or qualities that citizens in the fast-changing world of the 21st century need. They are explained further in Figure 4.2.

These PLTS sit alongside other key skills such as literacy and numeracy, particularly in the secondary sector in England.

Skill	What it Means in Practice for Pupils
Independent enquirers	More input from the pupils in terms of planning what they will do and how they might do it.
Creative thinkers	This means asking questions, identifying problems and generating possible solutions.
Reflective learners	This is the opportunity for the pupils to evaluate their own learning and also get feedback from others
Team workers	Pupils collaborate with each other in small groups.
Self-managers	Pupils take responsibility for their own learning and organize their time and the resources to be used effectively
Effective participators	They negotiate with each other and indicate a willingness to listen to the ideas of others and discuss issues of concern

Fig. 4.2: Personal, learning and thinking skill development as applied to pupils

Frequent opportunities occur for these skills to be developed within the teaching of topics or subjects. Some schools may even adjust their timetables and insert opportunities for skills-based lessons within the course of the normal school week.

In Wales, the publication of a Skills Framework (as they might be applied to the 3–19-year-old age range) document (DCELLS, 2008b) heralded the arrival of 'thinking skills' as a major component, alongside more predictable elements such as communication, numeracy and ICT skills. Other key skills remained in the background but are still considered to be important. These include problem-solving, working with others and improving one's own performance. In addition to Thinking Skills, the key skills of Communication, Numeracy and ICT are given plenty of prominence in this document.

The Welsh Assembly Government (WAG) wants to promote a 'Plan, Do and Reflect' model of the curriculum, which pre-supposes the pupil taking some ownership of the learning process. This is founded on the principle of providing pupils with a challenge to their learning, which can mean engaging in meaningful problem-solving activities.

There is a great deal of emphasis laid on children being encouraged and challenged to move on in their learning when they are developmentally ready.

The move away from a knowledge-based curriculum to a skills based one was driven by the need for reform in the eyes of the policy-makers in Wales. Ongoing improvements in standards, generated by earlier reforms, were seen to have stalled and it was hoped that this would provide fresh impetus. It appeared to be founded on some research-based evidence (PISA, 2006) that there were higher standards in areas such as literacy and numeracy in other countries of comparable size (e.g. Finland) that had also adopted a similar skills-based curriculum. These results were confirmed in more recent research (PISA, 2009).

Changes were made to the National Curriculum arrangements in all subject areas in placing much greater emphasis on the use of an enquiry-based approach to teaching and learning together with a re-writing of the level descriptors. In a subject like science, this has proved to be controversial, as the criteria (now based on skills) are more difficult to interpret with any degree of reliability. The publication of new National Curriculum arrangements in 2008 (DCELLS, 2008a) indicated a marked decrease in expectation in terms of knowledge and understanding with greater emphasis being placed on skills development.

In addition to the curriculum changes mentioned above, there have been a number of developments that have exerted considerable influence on the curriculum followed by pupils in the 14–19 age range. A desire to personalize learning has underpinned much of what is happening in Wales in a similar fashion to England. As long ago as 1988 the Higginson report (DES, 1988) had highlighted problems with too much early specialization, at the age of 14, resulting in a narrowing of the curriculum with traditional option choices that pupils in Year 9 made in the past. More recently, the Teaching and Learning Research Programme (TLRP) (2006) findings indicated that there was some evidence that A level subjects, NVQ courses and BTEC courses were being studied without any reference to an overarching rationale. There were also continuing problems with those school leavers who were not in education, training or employment. It was felt that a more modern, broadly based curriculum was needed for the 21st century. As a consequence of all of this, the Welsh Baccalaureate (a Welsh version of the International Baccalaureate) was introduced, as mentioned earlier in this chapter. This eventually evolved into a Core programme, which sits alongside existing GCSE courses in subject like English, maths and science. This core programme consists of essential skills such as communication, an individual investigation, work-related education, PSE, a team enterprise activity and a unit called 'Wales, Europe and the World'.

Summary

Any investigation into school improvement that might examine the influence of teachers inside the classroom with pupils on their learning or working with colleagues outside the classroom cannot ignore the policy context in which such learning processes take place. Many of the initiatives teachers become involved with will owe their origins, directly or indirectly, to the former government-funded policy initiatives in England.

This discussion of the policy context shows some differences in emphasis between educational policy in England and Wales in relation to curriculum development. For example, there is more attention paid to skills development in Wales and there are also concerted attempts being made to promote Welsh language development and Welsh culture (Curriculum Cymreig) in schools. However, in policy terms, there are many shared concerns (e.g. personalized learning). This is less than surprising given the fact that families containing school-age children might well move between the two countries and it would not be desirable for radically different education systems to be created.

Self-study Questions

1 If your school gains or has gained 'academy' status, what might be or are the implications for pupils, staff and parents?
2 What might be the advantages and disadvantages of a more skills-based curriculum as it currently applies to schools in Wales?
3 What might be the advantages and disadvantages of a more subject-based curriculum (placing more emphasis on knowledge and understanding) as it might currently apply to schools in England?
4 To what extent do you agree with the assertion made in the Rose review (DCSF, 2009) of the primary curriculum that 'subjects are essential but not sufficient'?
5 In relation to personalized learning:
    (i)   To what extent do you think pupils you teach take much notice of the learning targets that are set?
    (ii) Do the pupils consider they have ownership of these targets?
6 The Personal, Learning and Thinking Skills (QCDA, 2009) are intended to sit alongside functional skills such as literacy and numeracy.
    (i)   How effectively are these skills being developed in the pupils you teach?
    (ii) What reasons can you give to support your views?

5 School Improvement, School Culture and the Micro-Politics of Change

Introduction

The main purpose of this chapter is to discuss the notion of educational change within the wider context of school improvement, as it might apply to the classroom where the core of teaching and learning activities occur. Clearly not all change results in improvement and as such will always involve an element of risk. Durrant and Holden (2006) list some key ingredients for sustaining school improvement including collaboration, trust, dialogue, planning and leadership. Of these, trust is all important, both between staff and pupils and among the teachers themselves.

School improvement is certainly about 'doing things better' (Hoyle and Wallace, 2005) and not doing better things, which can often equate to radical change and result in confusion and consternation among practitioners. It is hard not to disagree with Hoyle and Wallace's view that the constant imposition of externally generated education policies severely limits the scope for transformation. In this respect, then, changes to practice with the aim of gradually improving learning at the classroom level is what really counts. It is worth mentioning that the coalition government in its white paper on education (DfE, 2010) indicated a move away from a target-driven, interventionist agenda for school improvement towards a position where the responsibility for improvement lies with schools themselves, attempting to 'make it easier for schools to learn from one another' (p.73).

Change itself can involve cultural and political elements. Organizational culture (Close and Raynor, 2010) in schools is always difficult to discuss as it exists in many different forms. Expectations of staff, pupils and parents play a key role in formulating school culture. However, all types of schools, particularly those in urban contexts, now have to cope with more and more cultural diversity.

Change itself, in terms of education policy, has always been highly political and often very contentious. Teachers are socialized both professionally (i.e. generally) and organizationally (i.e. in a specific school) into a profession that tries to uphold high standards of behaviour, but enforced change (whether driven by central government or by the SLT in a school) can often generate resistance (which can be implicit, unspoken and subversive) and may lead to different forms of conflict between staff.

Both the cultural and political dimensions of change necessary to drive school improvement form an important backdrop for the practical applications of teacher leadership, which are discussed in Chapters 7–10.

Change

It is axiomatic that the motivation, on the part of most teachers, for improving the quality of learning is the desire that all pupils might achieve their full potential. No improvement in the quality of teaching can occur without change, but not all change brings about improvement, particularly in terms of what might be readily measureable. In fact, many educational policy initiatives fail to be implemented effectively (Fullan, 1991), and often the main reasons for that are schools find themselves having to implement multiple initiatives almost simultaneously or the funding for an initiative is withdrawn after a short period before the consequent changes in practice have become fully embedded in practice. It is also the case that policy-makers often do not do enough to convince teachers of the need for change and can also neglect human agency. Human agency can be interpreted as the capacity of an individual or individuals to make a difference and is guided by a 'driving' moral purpose. Thus if the staff in a school become convinced of the need for change and the proposed change fits or is congruent with their model of educational beliefs collectively, this might then create the conditions in which change could be implemented successfully.

Fullan (1997) argued that a number of assumptions can easily be made about change, and he suggested that lessons can be learned about its successful implementation, which may be reinterpreted in the context of teacher-leaders. Four of these assumptions have been selected for further discussion below as being particularly relevant to teacher-leaders.

- Effective change takes time – significant change can take two or three years. This means that teacher-leaders need considerable patience and persistence when working with their colleagues, particularly in the early stages. This was reinforced by the MacBeath et al. (2007) research findings. They noted that short-term pressures will produce a culture of 'show-me-quick' results, which will be counter-productive in the longer term.
- Teacher-leaders need to tolerate a degree of uncertainty and ambiguity as individuals work through the change and begin to understand more about its meaning. Thus things will not improve immediately and in fact may actually get worse in the short term (implementation dip).
- Teacher-leaders should not expect everyone with whom they collaborate to change. If anything, it is better to focus on increasing the numbers of people that become supportive.
- Teacher-leaders should expect disagreement, as any change is bound to generate different viewpoints. Open and honest discussion conducted in a professional manner is a positive step forward in this process.

A Model of Teacher Change

Traditionally, continuing professional development (CPD) for teachers has often been implicitly based on the notion that some form of ad hoc training would change teachers' attitudes about classroom pedagogy before changes in pupil learning outcomes have been observed. Guskey (2002) challenged this conceptualization and proposed a model of change centred around the notion that teachers will only change their attitudes towards a change when they can see it working in the classroom. Such a model is based on two components:

- Teachers' pragmatism: they hope to gain some practical ideas from any CPD activity;
- Experiential learning: this is focused on the teachers' learning and is based on day-by-day observation, reflection and analysis of classroom practice. This aspect finds support from Earley and Bubb (2004), who stressed the importance of 'learning by doing, sharing, reviewing and applying' (p.18).

The model can be set out as follows:

CPD (A) ⟶ CHANGES IN PRACTICE (B) ⟶ CHANGES IN OUTCOMES (C) ⟶ CHANGES IN ATTITUDES (D)

Professional development (A) for teachers may involve training in the use of an innovative teaching technique (for example, use of formative assessment techniques). Changes in practice (B) may generate improved learning outcomes for pupils (C). Guskey argued that changes in teachers' attitudes (D) can then occur as a result of seeing what actually works in the classroom.

Guskey's model is presented as a linear one, but he felt that it is more likely to be cyclical. He acknowledged that it is difficult to change the attitudes of experienced teachers. He cited several studies in support of his argument to show that teachers experience anxiety and confusion in the initial period of implementation (B) before the problems begin to be ironed out. One of the possible strengths of this model is its ability to explain what really happens when change is introduced and why so much fails. However, it should be borne in mind that such a process may not apply to all staff and for some the changes in attitude may occur with changes in practice almost simultaneously.

School Improvement

According to Gray (2005), school improvement can manifest itself in three distinct but complementary ways: **tactical** (e.g. placing pupils on the grade C–D boundary under regular scrutiny to improve results); **strategic** (e.g. placing more emphasis on more analysis of current practice for more long-term improvement); and **capacity building** (which tries to involve as many staff as possible). It would be difficult to conceive of any form of school improvement being sustained without an investment in *social capital*, which according to Hargreaves (2001) is based on building up trust so that teachers collaborate effectively, encouraging networks to develop within the school itself. If a school is preparing for an inspection, this might help such networks to develop when preparing the self-evaluation information. Equally, trust between all stakeholders (teachers, pupils and parents) is clearly very important.

Durrant and Holden (2006) argued that school improvement is heavily dependent on top-down support for bottom-up change. Support from the SLT will obviously be dependent on whether the proposed change fits alongside the school development plan at that given time or whether it might need to be delayed for other reasons. Such support can take many different forms, including moral backing, authorizing any organizational changes that may be needed, clear encouragement on a personal level and providing advice in the face of difficulties.

It is not altogether clear why some schools improve the performance of pupils more than others, which is obviously one indicator of school improvement over time. Improving teaching methods and ensuring pupils learn more effectively is important because this is centred more closely on the idea of helping the child to achieve his or her full potential as far as learning outcomes are concerned. It is hard to disagree with Hopkins' (in DfES, 2005) claim that 'it is at the level of the individual classroom teacher that most of the differences between schools occur' (p.4).

At the start of the second decade of the 21st century, it has become apparent that government policy was allowing teachers more freedom to determine what was most appropriate for their pupils in terms of improving learning and raising achievement levels. This is reflected in the emphasis on personalized learning, which takes more account of diversity among the pupil population and their preferred ways of learning. This generated more opportunities for pupils to feel some ownership of their learning, both in primary and secondary schools.

However, school improvement is not unproblematic because, as Busher (2006) noted, it does imply that things are always getting better for everyone concerned, particularly the pupils. In reality this may not be the case, as some groups of pupils may benefit from their involvement in a particular initiative while others do not. If funding for school improvement projects is reduced or withdrawn, then further improvements in the standards of pupils' learning may not be sustained.

According to Durrant and Holden (2006), some initiatives might well be considered as being 'shallow', i.e. preoccupied with short-term, performance-driven outcomes. Others might lead to more profound, deeper changes in practice, for example, giving greater weight to 'learner voice' or placing far more emphasis on peer coaching or classroom-based enquiry. Such enquiry may well involve conducting some form of action research, which is always longer term and requires a more thoughtful, self-evaluative approach.

Taking Risks

Hughes (2002) asserted an important principle: teachers are more likely to make small changes to their classroom practice than drastic changes. He referred to this as 'tweaking', a step-by-step approach to change occurring over time. He argued that 'leaving the comfort zone involves risk' (p.25). Here the notion of risk is not being discussed in the context of health and safety concerns, but has more of focus on a teacher putting an idea about pedagogy into practice in the classroom for the first time, when the learning 'gain' may not be entirely predictable. In other words, traditional (tried-and-trusted) methods enable some learning to take place, but the use of an innovative approach might produce learning of a higher quality (e.g. in terms of developing a more in-depth understanding of the subject) than would be anticipated.

Risk-taking pre-supposes that a teacher-leader is willing to make changes to pedagogy in order to enhance learning. The risk lies in the fact that the experiment may not work and/or produce unintended outcomes. This willingness also includes emotional dimension, where increased stress on teachers can be the result of constant monitoring and too much emphasis being placed on accountability. Such an approach also assumes that an individual teacher has enough experience to have some idea to determine which initiatives are promising and which are likely to be less effective. Some proposed changes may not be enacted in practice as they are unaffordable or make too many demands on scarce resources, or the timing is not considered to be appropriate by the SLT.

Trust and respect are essential prerequisites for risks to be taken, between teachers and pupils and between teachers themselves. The creation of trust can lead to greater commitment and ownership, especially if fears and anxieties are allowed to be heard. This then can lead to what Harris (2004) called 'emotional fitness'. It is harder to take risks in schools that might be branded as failing or under-performing following an inspection. Staff can feel resentful if presented by the SLT with the opportunity to participate in educational initiatives that appear to offer unsustainable 'quick-fixes'. Harris argued that emotional fitness of staff is developed when self-esteem is raised, hope is restored, morale is raised and a sense of community is promoted. Above all, teachers need to feel that their efforts are being appreciated and their views are being taken into consideration.

It is more likely that risk-taking will take place if teachers are able to collaborate and work together in small groups. The best-known example of this is the IQEA project (Hopkins and Harris, 1997) where teachers are encouraged to investigate an aspect of classroom practice that is also of interest to several other teachers (e.g. challenging the able and talented pupils). Thus, in the 'cadre' formed, learning from each other in the workplace becomes an important driver in contributing to developing a culture of improving pupils' learning (Fullan, 2009).

As has already been stated, risk-taking is not entirely predictable: teachers have to decide on the degree of risk involved. Day-to-day teaching can incorporate opportunities for any number of relatively low-level risks to be taken (e.g. changing the seating arrangements so that certain pupils might learn better with other partners and be more focused on matters in hand).

Since education is a balance between using appropriate pedagogy (with a focus on learning processes) and producing desirable outcomes in terms of key data (e.g. exam results, Key Stage 1 and 2 assessments), any risk needs to judged by making a comparison with current teaching approaches and its likely effect on outcomes. A teacher who lacks self-confidence may well shy away from embarking on strategies perceived to be risky and be more 'conservative' in their pedagogy. It is also clear that risk-taking needs to be modelled by the SLT if teachers are to be encouraged to take risks themselves. Stoll and Temperley (2009) argued that if justifiable risks need to be taken then members of the SLT should lead by example for such practice to become the norm.

One justifiable risk that is always worthy of careful consideration is the extent to which pupils themselves have greater ownership in their learning and a greater say in how they choose to undertake their learning journey. Such an emphasis places 'pupil voice' at the heart of the debate and the pupils can exercise influence over what happens in classrooms. According to Harris (2007), 'teacher leadership of learning only makes sense within the context of student leadership of learning' (p.45). She then goes on to argue that student voice offers the opportunity 'to be a launch pad for more co-creative and enriching learning between students and teachers' (p.45).

To lead change and contribute to school improvement does presume that teacher-leaders have a well-developed understanding of the culture and micro-political processes that operate at different levels within a school, for example: (i) the school as a whole; (ii) the subject department in a secondary school or year group/Key Stage in a primary school and in the classroom; and (iii) in the classroom with pupils and support staff.

School Culture

School culture is socially constructed by all those who work in it, with some members being far more influential than others. It is exemplified and reinforced by a wide variety of practices such as ceremonies, rituals, rules, visual representations (for example, photographs of pupils who have achieved high standards of achievement in sport) as well as attitudes towards education that teachers might have (for example, deeply held beliefs about the importance of child-centred education). Thus the culture of a school – which can often be described as its ethos – is a complex mix of values and beliefs.

The whole school culture or ethos is usually shaped by the SLT. However, sub-cultures exist with the school's organizational culture, e.g. subject departments in secondary schools and year group teachers in primary schools. The term 'culture' does not have a widely agreed definition and it is easy to use terminology like 'a culture of learning' or a 'culture of achievement' without really questioning what such terms mean. Some guidance has been offered by Hoyle and Wallace (2005), who argued that it encapsulates 'values, beliefs, attitudes, opinions, norms, behaviour, language, institutions, artefacts, symbols, codes...' (p.113). Values are extremely important as they can act as a driving force for change (Busher, 2006). Such values can be discussed from a personal perspective and from a more collective point of view. Values are implicit and sub-conscious for teachers, which makes them difficult to articulate. Those the school might wish to promote might include democracy, integrity, respect, tolerance, curiosity, equality etc. The individual teacher lives his or her life in school in a 'field' of values (adapted from Hodgkinson, 1991), as illustrated in Figure 5.1. V1, V2 and V3 are the most directly relevant to the work of teacher-leaders.

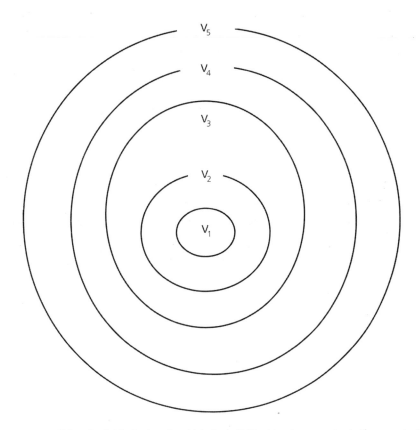

Fig. 5.1 Conceptualizing the field of values in which the individual teacher operates in the organizational culture of a school

V1   Personal values of individual staff
V2   Informal Group values (e.g. departmental in secondary school; year group staff in a primary school; pupils in a class)
V3   Whole school values at an organizational level

V4   Local community values shaped by LEA, parents, employers and the context in which the school is situated (i.e. urban, suburban or rural)

V5   National values incorporating the cultural 'spirit of the times' (*Zeitgeist*). This is referred to as the macro-culture.

Teacher leadership is founded on a set of congruent, informal group values (V2), which are usually assumed and implicit when teachers work together (e.g. loyalty, collegiality, commitment, trust). Building alliances with other staff to promote change is very important. The personal values (V1) are also subsumed within this construct. Differences in the attitudes and values held by individual members of the group can be tolerated if there are strong bonds between the group members.

Busher (2006) noted that values for pupils as a group (V2) ought to include respect, tolerance, democracy, building up pupils' self-esteem, trust etc., even though they might be described as being utopian. He included other core values for working with other staff, such as fairness, compassion, effectiveness, collaboration and support, sharing resources. At the boundary between V2 and V3 lies the notion of whole school support from the SLT, and especially the headteacher. It becomes more difficult to initiate change if there is an absence of support for teacher leadership.

Schools are situated in a wide variety of environmental contexts, such as urban, suburban and rural. Tensions might arise when the values espoused by the school are different from those held by some in the local community the school serves. This is particularly challenging for schools in inner-city areas, which exhibit a considerable degree of diversity. Riley (2009) painted a contrasting picture of urban life: contrast and disparity in relation to wealth; opportunity and restriction in relation to employment; location and dislocation between those who feel they belong and those on the margins of society. A rise in gang culture sits uneasily with the values the school might wish to promote. Riley argued strongly for the positive effects of developing trust between pupils and teachers as well as raising the aspirations of those pupils from disadvantaged communities.

Cultural Approaches to Classroom Learning

Each school creates its own unique approach to learning by promoting what is valued within the local school community. All schools are located in specific contextual ways (e.g. rural, urban) and it is most likely that a given classroom culture will reflect a whole school culture, which is set by all the relevant stakeholders (teachers, pupils and parents alike).

Busher (2006) argued that organizational culture can be represented in a whole host of different ways (e.g. through the use of symbolism and ritual). Teachers create their own sub-cultures in smaller working units. Sub-cultures exist both in primary and secondary schools, usually reflecting subject department interests in secondary schools or those of a specific year group in primary schools, where staff work in small teams (e.g. teachers for Years 1 and 2 as well as a teacher for a mixed class of Year 1 and 2 pupils). These are important for the study of teacher leadership in relation to teachers working with their colleagues. However, they can also be applied to classroom sub-cultures (Busher, 2006). Figure 5.2 illustrates how these sub-cultures might apply to teacher-leaders in the classroom. Classroom sub-cultures are very different for young children, where there are likely to be more teaching assistants and even nursery nurses for the youngest ones. In secondary schools, such sub-cultures are more fluid, as an individual teacher may belong to several different formal or informal groups.

Organizational Sub-Cultural Elements (Busher, 2006)	Application to Classroom Teachers Leading the Learning
Symbols and rituals	The ways pupils are grouped in a classroom; whether all groups of pupils have equal access to resources; primary teachers speaking to parents at the end of the school day; TAs helping SEN pupils.
Customs	These are linked strongly to behaviour. In small group discussions, one person speaking at a time and pupils being encouraged to listen to the views of other pupils.
Myths and beliefs	Beliefs about the teacher being a learner as well as the pupils; a belief in the effectiveness of a child-centred approach would mean focusing on what prior knowledge pupils have about a topic; pupils being actively involved in the construction of knowledge.
Images of the school	Work which is displayed celebrating the work of pupils in classrooms or can be displayed in the school foyer.
Language	Use of word walls for the enhancement of vocabulary; words printed and displayed in the Welsh language in Welsh schools to promote bilingual approaches to education.
Communication style	Use of written text; active discussion approaches such as 'think-pair-share' in small-group work; use of ICT including the IWB as a stimulus for discussion and feedback from pupils.
People and action	At a weekly assembly, an award is made to 'pupil of the week' in each class.
Stories of success or failure	Thinking about why the use of a specific approach either worked well or did not work; public celebration of achievements in assemblies.
Explicit rules	Classroom rules for behaviour clearly displayed on the walls of the classroom (discussed with pupils in some detail, with pupils also deciding what the appropriate sanction should be if the rules are broken).

Organizational Sub-Cultural Elements (Busher, 2006)	Application to Classroom Teachers Leading the Learning
Implicit rules	Very strongly linked to the moral values being modelled; e.g. respect, honesty, democracy, equity etc.
Organization sub-cultural elements (Busher, 2006)	Application to classroom teachers leading the learning
Goals	Learning targets, personalized to the needs of the individual pupil.
Characters played	Teacher and support staff play the role of motivator, encourager, social worker, facilitator and try to inspire pupils to persevere.

Fig. 5.2 Aspects of classroom sub-culture and their possible meaning for teacher-leaders at the classroom level

The Micro-Politics of Change

Here it is being assumed that any changes designed to bring about school improvement will have a political dimension, especially when a teacher-leader works with colleagues where the main emphasis is on collaboration and collegiality. In this context, there is usually a great deal of mutual interdependence. Yet to ignore micro-politics (i.e. the politics that operates within a school community) would not be advisable, given that so much of what teachers frequently do (either with pupils, other colleagues or parents) is based on negotiation, bargaining, conflict resolution and building coalitions. In general, it is rare to find examples of ongoing, open disagreement between staff in schools. Even though it is accepted that teachers will not always agree with each other, they would be expected to act professionally with other staff, pupils and parents. In addition, there is an expectation that the school will develop a sense of community, giving due recognition to the diverse contributions to 'school life' by all those who work in the school, and there would be regular opportunities to share values among all the participants.

There are several assumptions that are made here. The first is that political perspectives are as much about respecting the differences of opinion that emerge between teachers as they are about staff reaching consensus and engaging in collaborative activities. Teacher-leaders live in a school community characterized by rules, customs, traditions and shared interests. Therefore they can play a pivotal role in policy interpretation and also influence decision-making processes. Such interpretation of policy is often a contested area of debate among teachers.

The second assumption is that micro-political strategies are essentially learned through the work context (i.e. what they are and how to use them). Inevitably, teacher-leaders would rely on exercising very good interpersonal skills, which might involve diplomacy, self-control (especially of one's own emotions) and offers of empathetic support when appropriate.

According to Bacharach (1988), schools are political systems where power struggles take place in an effort to obtain control over resources. Participants become political actors with their own needs objectives and strategies. Decision making is the main arena of conflict. Participation may depend on self-interest, i.e. actors engage in discussions to get the decision they want. Sub-groups exist, each of which has a different view on who has the formal power (delegated authority), informal power (influence) and who will make the decisions. At the classroom level, the formal authority of a teacher might be rejected by the pupils if that teacher is perceived as being 'weak' or 'soft'. This can lead to loss of control, particularly of classroom discipline, and mean that the teacher exerts very little influence on learning. However, if the pupils choose to accept the teacher's authority, then that teacher can be influential in terms of motivating and inspiring pupils to engage constructively in the learning process.

The ability of an individual or group to have its interests represented in the decision-making process may be limited. Larger coalitions or alliances may emerge that can decide or agree on desired objectives. They can then formulate strategies to achieve them (Bolman and Deal, 1994). Some coalitions can become more dominant than others within an individual school.

According to Busher (2006) teachers may use power to promote their perceptions of preferred and desirable policies and practice in school. They also consciously or sub-consciously personify values and exemplify a spiritual and moral framework that can be 'projected' to pupils and colleagues. Busher argued that teachers use a variety of micro-political strategies to achieve compliance rather than resistance from pupils and also seek to influence their colleagues in ways that fit their own perceptions of what should be happening These strategies include negotiating and bargaining; forming alliances or coalitions; collaborating on a give-and-take basis; actively being involved in decision-making; and dealing effectively with conflict. While educational policy is usually determined by the government, its implementation at the classroom level is sometimes a matter of debate and even controversy.

Busher (2006) proposed a useful model of the political features of a school as an organization that exists on three levels. Level 1: manifestations of power, which for teacher-leaders means exerting influence on pupils and other colleagues. Level 2: organizational groups and coalitions, which may be formalized, e.g. there are strongly overlapping areas of interest that bind teachers together in a subject department in a secondary school or in a the same year group or Key Stage in a primary school. They could also be informal groups or factions formed by members who socialize together a great deal and could also involve networks, which might be formed among staff who are working together as part of a school improvement project. Level 3: processes of negotiations, which are mainly concerned with operating in a social and cultural framework, establishing norms and values, using various strategies in particular locations, e.g. with pupils in a classroom

Blasé and Anderson (1995) commented on the ways in which teachers construct a political self-image consisting of two dimensions, one being based on a positive, proactive desire to be influential and a more negative, reactive desire to protect themselves in case their actions could be misinterpreted. The latter arises because an individual teacher's actions are the subject of continuous comment and scrutiny by pupils, parents and other teachers. Blasé and Anderson also pointed out that when considering interactions with other staff, there is a good deal of emphasis on support. The politics of support involves being diplomatic; controlling one's own emotions; showing friendliness towards work colleagues; offering support in terms of sharing resources.

To help explain why teacher-leaders are effective, it may be that they have learned to manage successfully the micro-politics by using an appropriate range of strategies with pupils, parents and colleagues. Examples of the strategies that might be used could be: negotiating; bargaining/resolving disagreements; involvement in decision-making (Turner, 2009).

When teacher-leaders work with pupils in the classroom, whole-class debates provide a chance for more fundamental values to be promoted (e.g. showing respect for the opinions of others; listening to those who you may disagree with; giving different people the opportunity to express an opinion etc.). Class discussion is an extremely important tool for promoting learning. In this context, teachers manage the boundary between what is acceptable behaviour and what is not. It does reflect the kind of moral dilemma facing many teachers almost daily, i.e. the desire to have an open discussion of interest to the pupils balanced with not allowing other pupils or even staff to be verbally abused. This is tied in with the values that staff wish to promote (Busher, 2006). Busher argued that power is manifest in relation to the influence the teacher-leader can bring to bear. This is particularly true when it comes to decision-making. From a micro-political perspective, this may be concerned with addressing questions such as: Who makes the decisions? On what basis? Are any alliances being formed between the teacher-leader and other colleagues? To what extent is a teacher-leader able to voluntarily operate a power-sharing democratic strategy, especially in relation to negotiating what is learned and how it is learned, in the best interests of the pupils? This can involve allowing pupils more ownership of their own learning, which represents a power shift in terms of the classroom dynamics.

The extent of the influence a teacher-leader can have is clearly dependent on the working context, the teacher's positional status and reputation in the school and the designated responsibilities that teacher carries. However, Harris and Muijs (2005) noted in their research that even relatively young and inexperienced teacher-leaders could be successful as political leaders. Given that most teachers are 'unaccustomed to expressing open disagreement directly to those with whom they disagree' (Schmuck and Runckel, 1994, p.329), it would appear that placing a reliance on negotiation and bargaining to gain acceptance would be more productive rather than increasing resistance by appearing to be inflexible. This applies to staff, pupils and parents.

Part of the negotiations with pupils is concerned with managing the boundaries because it reflects on the values teacher-leaders are trying to emphasize with pupils. These include respect and empathy.

It should be noted that it is difficult for teacher-leaders to discuss their political struggles with other staff, possibly because of the over-arching culture of collegiality, which dominates teachers' thinking about professionalism.

Summary

Observing gradual improvements in the quality of pupils' learning is a very important motivator for teachers and an essential part of their job satisfaction. This is a complex, messy process involving a willingness to embrace change and take risks. This is perhaps the most interesting aspect of the implementation of change. Any element of risk means that the teacher is moving out of his or her 'comfort zone' and collaborative work can mean persuading other staff to do the same. It also means dealing with the unintended outcomes arising from the introduction of the change as well as the possibility of failure.

Teacher-leaders can never guarantee improved pupil learning outcomes and Guskey's (2002) model does raise some interesting questions about the ways in which teachers' attitudes are shaped by the implementation of innovative pedagogical approaches.

The existence of sub-cultures is self-evident in schools (e.g. in departments in secondary schools based on the teaching of subject or year groups in primary schools based on teaching pupils in a particular age range). Differences between staff will emerge and thus there will always be an important political dimension to any sort of collaboration between staff. A classroom culture that celebrates success as well as placing an emphasis on personalized learning is likely to produce pupils with very positive attitudes to learning.

It is clear that values place a vital role in driving change and teacher-leaders will epitomize those values as much as anything by the way they behave. Values such as curiosity, tolerance, honesty and respect are lived out on a day-by-day basis by the teacher who can then model them for pupils. If a school sets a high value on inclusiveness, then the children will quickly pick up on this, and can then learn more about tolerating pupils who may come from very disadvantaged backgrounds or have very specific special needs. When teachers work closely with other staff, inevitably disagreements arise. These are inevitable in organizations like schools and effective teacher-leaders will know how to balance all the competing demands made upon them in the current climate of individual and collective accountability.

Self-study Questions

1 (i)   What higher risk strategies have you used in your classroom teaching recently?
   (ii) To what extent did you involve other teachers in discussions about what you were planning to do?
2 Think about a change you have been involved with recently. Refer back to the four assumptions about change in this chapter. How applicable are these four assumptions to the change you are thinking about? For example, has it been given sufficient time to be implemented?
3 Busher (2006) argued that teachers should demonstrate desirable personal values (e.g. trust, tolerance [V1 in Figure 5.1]) and group values (such as collaboration, sharing resources [V2 in Figure 5.1]). How do you think these values can be enacted in practice most effectively?
4 With reference back to Figure 5.2:
   (i)   How would you characterize the sub-culture in your own classroom?
   (ii) Which elements are especially applicable?
5 To what extent do you think micro-political issues have any real relevance to:
   (i)   classroom practice?
   (ii) collaborative work done with your colleagues?
6 Why do you think it is so difficult to convince experienced teachers who are successful in terms of their classroom teaching and learning of the need to make changes to their classroom practice?

6 Background to the Research

Introduction

The next four chapters (7–10) contain evidence collected from practitioners working in primary and secondary schools in England and Wales. This is presented and based upon a framework of ideas about teacher leadership, which is the analytical tool used in this book. The two main purposes of this chapter, therefore, are:

(i) To set out for the reader how the research was set up and conducted;
(ii) To describe the sample in as much detail as possible without compromising confidentiality and anonymity.

Schools Situated in Different Contexts

Urban schools are characterized by ever-increasing complexity and diversity. Riley (2009) contrasted the situation between pupils who live in relatively affluent areas with plenty of support at home and only a relatively short distance away from less well-to-do areas, characterized by poverty, financial pressures on parents etc., which can produce pupils who have low expectations of themselves and high levels of disaffection. Riley highlighted the importance of building trust between schools and their pupils and parents residing in such disadvantaged locations, which act as a 'glue' holding a school community together. Teachers obviously contribute to this, both in their dealings with pupils, parents and other teachers. Building the school's internal sense of community is clearly important. Connecting with the local community also means developing ethical and moral leadership and begins to address issues concerning social justice and sustainability. The challenges to be met in a school located in an urban area are to some extent shaped by the diverse nature of their clientele, especially in relation to asylum seekers, pupils coming from backgrounds where English is not their first language and economic migrants. However, the evidence presented by Muijs and Harris (2007) appears to suggest that teacher leadership can flourish even in urban schools serving socially disadvantaged estates.

Suburban schools are, by definition, to be found in areas away from the city centre, usually in more pleasant, residential locations. They often serve local estates, but staff working in these schools do not normally face the same degree of challenge experienced by their colleagues in urban schools. However, even in these areas, suburban schools are not immune to the effects of marital breakdown or economic uncertainty caused by a reduction in employment opportunities at the present time.

Rural schools are not necessarily sited in or near towns, but their size is dependent on the size of the community they draw upon. They can serve communities in decline because of the closure of traditional industries. They often struggle in terms of maintaining a viable school roll and tensions can arise if there are proposed closures or amalgamations with other local schools, usually driven by local authorities who are struggling to cope with budget cuts and wish to introduce more economies of scale.

The Research Design

This was set up to investigate more about how teacher-leaders perceived themselves (and how they were perceived by others) as building and maintaining a culture of collaboration and shared values in their efforts to lead the learning of pupils in the classroom as well as trying to find out more how they attempted to ensure that all the pupils they taught learned effectively. Similarly, questions were used to find out about the extent of their collaboration with colleagues to promote pupils' learning. Their present or recent involvement with school improvement initiatives was discussed. This was considered to be important because it represents a clear intention to improve pupils' learning directly or indirectly as a result of, for example, using targeted interventions to raise the standards of pupils' literacy and numeracy.

Engaging with parents with a focus on their child's learning was also considered to be part of this investigation into teacher leadership. It was assumed that a focus on pupil learning resulted from an active partnership between the school, the pupil and the parents, even if, in some cases, that vital support from home was not always forthcoming.

An additional dimension with the research design was to see if it was possible to find some degree of corroboration with the classroom teachers' views on teacher leadership by questioning one member of the SLT. It was important to discover how the concept of distributed leadership was interpreted, which would then indicate the extent of whole school support for teacher leadership. Finding out about decision-making, in the context of distributed leadership, would also help in this respect. As well as investigating the extent to which pupils were encouraged to lead their learning, an attempt was made to find whether any barriers to the development of teacher collaboration existed that could limit their influence when working with their colleagues.

Research Methodology

When deciding on the best way of finding out the answer to the following two questions:

(i)   How do teacher-leaders lead learning in their classrooms?

(ii) How do teacher-leaders influence their colleagues to try and improve pupils' learning?

it seemed appropriate to employ a case study approach, which would yield a useful set of data. According to Yin (2003), such a choice is justifiable when 'a "how or why" question is being asked about a contemporary set of events over which the investigator has little or no control' (p.9). Yin argued that a case study is 'an empirical enquiry which investigates a contemporary phenomenon within its real-life context' (p.13). In this research, case studies were chosen where the unit of analysis was the teacher, first and foremost, rather than the school. This was helpful because the theoretical ideas about teacher leadership could then be applied to real-life contexts. One obvious assumption being made here is that all teachers and schools are unique: they operate in different circumstances with pupils from a wide variety of backgrounds. The teachers and support staff also originate from different backgrounds and bring to the school a wide range of skills and experience. Some schools also operate in very challenging circumstances with large numbers of pupils coming from very deprived home backgrounds. The case study approach allows some detailed description, reflection and analysis to be carried out. It can provide rich data that is difficult to obtain in other ways.

Several approaches were considered as to the best ways of collecting data on the work of teachers. Questionnaires might have been created in order to obtain the information, but the use of such methods is always limited by the number and complexity of the questions used. It is also worth bearing in mind that time is needed for busy teachers to sit down and complete such an instrument.

A more in-depth, qualitative approach to the research was adopted. Semi-structured interviews were employed because they allowed staff to talk about the ways they might exercise teacher leadership and the interviewer (the author) to ask follow-up questions in order to clarify their responses. The questions were sent to the staff involved in advance to give them time to think and prepare their ideas and to present them in ways that sounded sensible. However, for various reasons, not all the staff received a copy of the questions before the interviews took place.

This process was only able to start with the agreement of headteachers in the schools who responded positively to the invitation to be involved. In the first instance, a wide range of schools in the primary and secondary sectors in England and Wales were contacted by letter. Headteachers were asked to nominate two effective classroom practitioners and one member of the Senior Leadership Team (SLT) to be interviewed about their work. The questions focused on their interactions with pupils and their collaborative efforts with other staff, the common denominator being the influence on the quality of pupil learning. The use of two teacher-leaders to be interviewed removed the possibility of analyzing a unique case, which would inevitably mean the data was less than robust.

The boundaries of any case study approach need to be carefully delineated (Hitchcock and Hughes, 1995). The headteachers were asked to nominate two effective classroom practitioners as teacher-leaders within their school. A set of criteria accompanied the letter to help them make that selection. The possible criteria included:

- the person chosen would have taught for more than five years and would have gone through threshold process;
- the person selected may be in possession of a formal post of responsibility for which the individual member of staff *might* or *might not* have a TLR (paid post of responsibility for teaching and learning);
- the person might have had the quality of his or her teaching assessed as good or better by the inspectorate – i.e. Ofsted (in England) and Estyn (in Wales) – recently.

The selection of two teachers from the same school gave an opportunity to carry out some cross-case analysis within the same school and the collection of data from schools in different contexts also gave the opportunity for cross-case analysis across schools.

Case studies themselves are not beyond some critical comment. According to Cohen et al. (2007), they may give a misleading impression, as some important evidence might have been overlooked; they can be rather anecdotal; and can also be very bland in the uncritical portrayal of the views of the interviewees. Clearly, one case means that generalizations become meaningless. They have three inherent weaknesses (according to Cohen et al. 2007):

(i)   It is difficult to draw conclusions based on cause and effect. However, any number of factors might influence teachers and pupils in the 'messy' process of learning.
(ii) There is a potential for bias, as teachers were asked to draw upon their memory of events that have been taking place recently and an individual teacher's memory may be very selective and may have an in-built level of unreliability;
(iii) The comments made by teachers could be largely superficial and impressionistic.

Face-to-face semi-structured interviews have certain intrinsic strengths and weaknesses. The strengths are related to the depth of the responses given by the interviewee, who can add more detail and explain his or her answer, if necessary. Questions can be rephrased if not fully understood by the respondent. The weaknesses can be reflexive, i.e. telling the interviewer what the interviewee thinks he or she wants to hear; plus they can be hampered by poor recall or poor preparation, leading to an unsatisfactory account. The reliability was improved by sending the transcripts of the interviewees back to them for checking. This allowed the respondents to remove any comments that were expressed inadequately and insert other aspects that were omitted from the original interview.

The Sample

A range of primary and secondary schools in England and Wales were contacted by letter, which explained the purposes of the research, and the headteachers were then asked if they wished to take part. This initial procedure was adopted on the assumption that every school has some teacher-leaders who would be recognized as effective classroom practitioners and to exert some degree of pedagogical influence among their colleagues. It was essential that all the primary schools contacted had a school roll of at least 200 pupils, which would then mean that for a given teacher-leader, there would be at least 8 other colleagues with whom they could collaborate, as well as a number of support staff.

Most of the schools contacted failed to reply to the letter inviting them to participate in this investigation. This was not unexpected, as there are many day-to-day pressures on schools, which they have to manage. There can be many requests from central or local government personnel to occupy the attention of headteachers, sometimes in terms of the implications of outcome 'data' that indicate the standards achieved by pupils in a given cohort (e.g. National Curriculum levels).

Of those schools that did respond, there was sufficient number to generate a useful sample, although it proved *extremely* difficult to persuade enough primary schools in England to participate. Among the reasons for this were impending inspections, staff absence, the absence of funding to cover supply costs, the continuing implications of the recently introduced policy of 'rarely cover' or being already involved in a research project with another HE institution. Ultimately, a total of 16 schools was selected as a suitable sample for this research. They were situated in England and Wales in rural, suburban and urban contexts. This total consisted of four primary and four secondary schools in England and the same numbers in Wales. Unfortunately, one of the primary schools in England that volunteered to participate in the investigation would only allow an interview with the deputy headteacher because of the 'rarely cover' obligations. After a great deal of deliberation, it was decided not to include the data from this school, as no teacher-leaders could be interviewed.

Tables 6.1–6.2 give details of the secondary schools used in England and Wales in the sample. The relative size of each school is indicated, using an arbitrary scale where small < 600 pupils; medium > 600 and < 1200 pupils; and large > 1200 pupils.

Name Of School	Location	Age Range	Size
Valley	Rural	11–18	Medium
Hillside	Suburban	11–18	Large
Waters Edge	Suburban	11–18	Large
Eastside	Urban	11–18	Large

Table 6.1 Details of the Welsh secondary schools used in the research

Name Of School	Location	Age Range	Size
Grange	Urban	11–16	Medium
Quarry	Suburban	11–16	Large
Beehive	Rural	11–18	Large
Crescent	Suburban	11–18	Large

Table 6.2 Details of the English secondary schools used in the research

Similarly, Tables 6.3–6.4 give details of the primary schools used in England and Wales in the sample. The relative size of each school is indicated, using an arbitrary scale where small < 200 pupils; medium > 200 and < 400 pupils; and large > 400 pupils.

Name Of School	Location	Age Range	Size
Avenue	Suburban	3–11	Large
Bridge	Urban	3–11	Large
Green	Rural	4–11	Large
Central	Urban	3–11	Medium

Table 6.3 Details of the Welsh Primary schools used in the research

Name Of School	Location	Age Range	Size
Galaxy	Urban	3–11	Large
Ashacre	Rural	4–11	Medium
Manor	Suburban	3–11	Medium

Table 6.4 Details of the English primary schools used in the research

Tables 6.5–6.8 show the relevant details for each classroom teacher and each member of the school's SMT interviewed in each primary and secondary school used in the research in England and Wales. It should be noted that it was only possible to interview one teacher-leader and one member of the SLT in Beehive Secondary School in England.

Four teachers included in the sample were selected by the member of the SLT in their respective schools despite their relative inexperience (i.e. they had not taught for five years or more). Nonetheless, they were selected on the basis of being effective classroom practitioners who were able to exercise some degree of influence with their colleagues in matters pertaining to teaching and learning.

Ethical Issues

The guidelines issued by British Education Research Council (BERA) (2004) were strictly adhered to. All the interviewees were willing volunteers. Permission was obtained to record the interviews from all respondents and guarantees were given assuring them of anonymity and confidentiality. As a result, all the names of the schools and individual staff have been changed.

Name of school	Avenue	Avenue	Avenue	Bridge	Bridge	Bridge
Teacher name	Sally	Ann	Laura	David	John	Sheila
Post(s) of responsibility	Member of the school's SLT	Team Leader for KS2	Team Leader for Foundation Phase	Science Co-ordinator; member of the SLT	Team Leader for KS2	Headteacher
Time in present post (years)	1	1	1	2	2	9
Length of time in present school (years)	11	4	3	12	11	11
Number of other schools worked in	0	1	3	4	1	2
Length of time in teaching (years)	11	7	10	>30	11	34
Number of full-time staff worked with	8	14	3	15	15	All
Number of part-time staff worked with	4	2	0	1	0	10
Number of support staff worked with	6	3	7	1	3	15

Table 6.5(i) Teacher details for those interviewed who work in primary schools in Wales

Name of school	Green	Green	Green	Central	Central	Central
Teacher name	Gillian	Jane	Gaynor	Christine	Ken	Lesley
Post(s) of responsibility	School Improvement Leader for KS2	Early Years and KS1 Team Leader	Headteacher	Assistant Headteacher	Year 5 and 6 Team Leader	Year 5 class teacher
Time in present post (years)	1/3	2/3	3	4	3	3
Length of time in present school (years)	14	7	3	28	9	3
Number of other schools worked in	3	1	4	4	0	0
Length of time in teaching (years)	16	13	>30	>30	9	3
Number of full-time staff worked with	2	4	All	All	4	1
Number of part-time staff worked with	1	0	3	4	1	0
Number of support staff worked with	2	3	18	30	8	2

Table 6.5 (ii) Teacher details for those interviewed who work in primary schools in Wales

Name of school	Valley	Valley	Valley	Eastside	Eastside	Eastside
Teacher name	Elizabeth	Natasha	Jason	Richard	Rhodri	Katie
Post(s) Of Responsibility	Head of Geography	Deputy Headteacher	Head of Maths	Head of Geography; seconded to SLT for 1 year	Deputy Headteacher	Head of MFL
Time in present post (years)	2	5	2	5	9	5
Length of time in present school (years)	4	5	14	14	27	27
Number of other schools worked in	0	2	1	0	2	0
Length of time in teaching (years)	4	25	14	14	>30	27
Number of full-time staff worked with	3	All	3	4	All	6
Number of part-time staff worked with	0	2	9	0	8	2
Number of support staff worked with	10	20	5	1	10	2

Table 6.6(i) Teacher details for those interviewed who work in secondary schools in Wales

Name of school	Waters Edge	Waters Edge	Waters Edge	Hillside	Hillside	Hillside
Teacher name	Gareth	Samantha	Gordon	Sian	Chris	Zoe
Post(s) Of Responsibility	Deputy Headteacher	Progress Leader for Year 8	KS4 Co-ordinator for English	Deputy Headteacher	Head of PE; [Head of Year 12]	Head of English
Time in present post (years)	9	4	1	9	14 [2]	4
Length of time in present school (years)	17	8	3	9	20	6
Number of other schools worked in	1	0	0	5	0	1
Length of time in teaching (years)	24	8	3	>30	20	10
Number of full-time staff worked with	All	15	20	All	17	10
Number of part-time staff worked with	0	8	1	20	1	2
Number of support staff worked with	30	6	0	35	5	0

Table 6.6(ii) Teacher details for those interviewed who work in secondary schools in Wales

Name of school	Galaxy	Galaxy	Galaxy	Ashacre	Ashacre	Ashacre
Teacher name	Jill	Fiona (1) Steve (2)	Karen	Kathleen	Janet	Thomas
Post(s) Of Responsibility	Headteacher	History Co-ordinator (1); Art Co-ordinator (2);	Maths Co-ordinator; Year 6 class teacher	Year 2 class teacher	Art Co-ordinator; Year 3 class teacher	Headteacher
Time in present post (years)	5	20 (1) 3 (2)	2	12	18	8
Length of time in present school (years)	5	12 (1) 3 (2)	2	12	18	8
Number of other schools worked in	5	3 (1) 0 (2)	2	4 (as TA)	0	5
Length of time in teaching (years)	28	20 (1) 3 (2)	8	12	18	26
Number of full-time staff worked with	All	6 (1) 1 (2)	1	2	3	All
Number of part-time staff worked with	2	1 (1) 1 (2)	1	2	1	6
Number of support staff worked with	14	2 (1) 2 (2)	2	2	3	25

Table 6.7(i): Teacher details for those interviewed who work in primary schools in England

Name of school	Manor	Manor	Manor
Teacher name	Simon	Natalie	Angella
Position of responsibility	Deputy Headteacher	Year 4 class teacher	Year 5 class teacher
Time in present post	½	1	9
Length of time in present school	2	1	10
Number of other schools worked in	2	0	1
Length of time in teaching	8	2	13
Number of full-time staff worked with	All	2	2
Number of part-time staff worked with	0	0	1
Number of support staff worked with	10	3	3

Table 6.7 (ii) Teacher details for those interviewed who work in primary schools in England

Name of school	Grange	Grange	Grange	Quarry	Quarry	Quarry
Teacher name	Pam	Sonia	Charles	Heather	Michael	Caroline
Position of responsibility	Head of History	Acting Head of Music	Deputy Headteacher	Teaching and Learning Consultant	Deputy Headteacher	Teaching and Learning Consultant
Time in present post	7	½	2	3	¾	3
Length of time in present school	9	4	12	6	¾	13
Number of other schools worked in	0	1	0	0	8	0
Length of time in teaching	9	5	12	6	12	13
Number of full-time staff worked with	5	10	15	10	All	50
Number of part-time staff worked with	0	1	2	3	30	4
Number of support staff worked with	3	1	0	8	50	16

Table 6.8(i) Teacher details for those interviewed who work in secondary schools in England

Name of school	Beehive	Beehive	Crescent	Crescent	Crescent
Teacher name	Paul	Jill	Suzie	Robert	Claire
Position of responsibility	Assistant Headteacher	AST (MFL)	AST (Acting) in English	AST; Head of Geography	Assistant Headteacher
Time in present post	2	4	1	3	1
Length of time in present school	6	9	11	4	9
Number of other schools worked in	1	2	0	0	1
Length of time in teaching	8	13	11	4	15
Number of full-time staff worked with	20	20	15	8	All
Number of part-time staff worked with	5	6	2	1	10
Number of support staff worked with	10	3	2	4	20

Table 6.8(ii) Teacher details for those interviewed who work in secondary schools in England

Prelude

Each of the next four chapters presents the findings from the interviews carried out with nominated staff in schools. The rationale for the way in which the data is presented is as follows:

(i)   It was felt to be important to discuss the extent to which the member of the SLT interviewed perceived that leadership was distributed in their school. One of the key indicators of distributed leadership is the degree to which all stakeholders may participate in the school's decision-making processes. The stakeholders include all the teaching staff, the support staff, the pupils and the parents.

(ii)   School improvement may be considered as being a crucial target outcome of any real exercise of teacher leadership. School improvement can be conceptualized as being a 'bottom-up' approach based on improving teaching and learning at the classroom level. To bring about improvement depends largely on teachers' determination to initiate changes in their pedagogy. It is also the case that government policy directives can also enforce changes in practice as well. It was accepted that not all the changes being introduced or that were being trialled would be successful, but there did need to be some evidence that teachers were willing to take some justifiable risks in order to secure longer-term improvements. Such efforts would also require active and ongoing support from the SLT. The views of a member of the SLT from each school and those of two nominated effective classroom practitioners about their involvement in educational initiatives are represented and discussed.

(iii)   Given that one of the two distinct dimensions of teacher leadership is about leading the learning in the classroom, the views of classroom teachers working with their pupils are discussed alongside SLT perspectives on the ways in which pupils can lead their own learning and gradually become more independent as learners themselves. The other dimension of teacher leadership is concerned with teachers collaborating with other colleagues (i.e. teachers and support staff). Evidence is presented here in the form of the teachers' views as to what might be effective when working with colleagues. At the same time, there are a number of potential barriers to teacher collaboration, and the views of the SLT are included in this section, to give a whole school perspective.

(iv)   In the final section, the perceptions of the work done by classroom teachers in partnership with the parents of the pupils they teach are presented.

Part 2
Practice

Leading the Learning in Primary Schools in England

Distributed Leadership: SLT Perspectives

(i) Manor Primary School

Simon, the deputy headteacher, noted that staff made contributions to whole school decisions on occasions. However, the SLT did have to make the final decisions on all matters. The support staff contributed in their curriculum team and had an equal voice. In many of the newly established curriculum teams, the support staff outnumbered the teachers. The participation of pupils in decision-making took place on an annual basis when they were surveyed and the results were often used to justify the decisions that were made to the pupils.

(ii) Galaxy Primary School

Jill, the headteacher, felt that hers had been a difficult transition from the previous incumbent when taking over as headteacher. There had previously been little delegation and a great deal of effort was made to enable subject co-ordinators to recognize that they were responsible and accountable for teaching and learning in their subject. The culture had changed slowly as some staff were able to adapt to the new challenge quickly but others had found the change more difficult and were insecure.

A major catalyst for change had been a subject inspection for design and technology in the second year of Jill's tenure. The inspector had spent about half an hour with Jill going through the online data and then the rest of the day with the subject leader for design and technology, observing lessons. This had a big impact as it reinforced the necessity for the 'subject leaders to take responsibility' message from Jill.

Jill used another tactic to involve other more senior staff in developing a more holistic view of the school:

> When we have the core meetings with the School Improvement Officer I wanted different members of the Senior Management Team to come into those meetings with myself, the

School Improvement officer and governors so that they would have an understanding of the whole strategic view of the school.

A number of new teachers who were relatively inexperienced subject leaders were now being supported by more experienced staff and the leadership was now far more distributed than it was previously.

Jill noted some decisions needed to be made without engaging staff in endless discussions. However, where things were open for discussion, then others could have their say, as appropriate. Support staff had a great deal of autonomy regarding their own work. They had less impact on whole school strategic decision-making as they did not attend staff meetings, although they attend INSET days.

(iii) Ashacre Primary School

Thomas, the headteacher, considered that leadership was now far more distributed than it was under the previous regime, but there was still room for improvement. In the most recent Ofsted inspection in 2009, one of the key issues was for the quality of delegated leadership to improve. This specifically mentioned the UPS3 (upper pay scale) staff who had not fully embraced their delegated leadership function. The school had also recently joined an informal partnership with another local authority school to share expertise and resources. One of the aims of this partnership was to help strengthen middle leadership development. Ashacre primary school was recognized as having particular strengths in the ways it educated SEN pupils whereas the other partner school was acknowledged to be well versed in developing its middle leaders.

The headteacher argued that the school had moved forward with the introduction of the 'Creative Curriculum' with its six areas of learning (as recommended by the Rose review [DCSF, 2009] and listed in Figure 4.1 in Chapter 4). Each of those areas was led by a UPS3 member of staff with teachers working together in each area. Such changes had been driven by the previous government's policies and performance management. However, Thomas noted that not all the curriculum requirements were subject based and fell outside the areas of learning: for example, community cohesion and being responsible for the gifted and talented.

There were always at least two TAs present at staff meetings and they had equal voting rights. Sometimes the TAs had meetings with their line managers or the SENCO (Special Educational Needs Co-ordinator). Recent developments had tended to focus on the effectiveness of the TA's work whereby they needed to feed back on the ways they felt they were having an impact on pupils' learning. There was a greater emphasis on developing pupils' independence as a result of teaching the pupils more about how to learn.

Pupils had an active role in making decisions, for example, in helping to design the new school uniform. School council representatives were able to interview the candidates for a recent SENCO post. Thomas explained their involvement in the following way:

When we interviewed for the SENCO the first time, they met the school council and we left the candidates with the school council. The children could ask them almost anything without us being there. The result was: we do not like any of them. We had to re-advertise.

Interviewer: Did the pupils get any training on the questions they might ask them and how they might ask them?

Yes. They have training on how they might ask. How might you find out something you are interested in? What do you think is important that somebody in this job does? ... When we interviewed the three candidates, we expected to be able to appoint one of them. There were two strong candidates, while one of them was an outsider. But actually, we agreed with the pupils.

Interviewer: So it was re-advertised, was it?

Yes, and the pupils were still involved the second time. The result was all the stakeholders, staff, pupils, governors agreed on the final choice. It was unanimous.

School Improvement: Recent Involvement in Educational Initiatives

(i) Manor Primary School

According to Simon, the deputy headteacher, a customized version of 'Skills for Life' had been developed by the staff in the school. These eight skills meant that the pupils should be able to plan, persevere, collaborate, develop empathy, be creative, have good management skills, be responsible and be able to show patience. It was intended that these would develop well in their time in the school. With their teacher's help, the pupils could come up with five 'I can ...' statements directly related to collaboration, for example. The pupils would then choose which statement was best suited to them for each skill.

In addition, the curriculum had been reorganized into six areas of learning, which had overcome the problem of subject co-ordinators working in isolation. Subjects were now grouped together under new banners and staff re-designated into teams. These teams were: the 'Culture' team, including art, RE, music and languages; the 'Wellbeing' team, including PSHE and PE; the 'Science and Technology' team; the 'Changes in Our World' team, including geography, history and the Eco-Schools initiative; the 'Mathematics' team and the 'English and Communication' team. It was a much more skills-based curriculum than had previously been the case and had taken into account the recommendations of the Rose report (DSCF, 2009). It had taken about one year of consultation to finally get the agreement of all the stakeholders to these new arrangements. All the existing staff were able to opt into a team of their choice. Support staff were allocated to a specific team and each team had its own budget to work within. A number of the more traditional staff meetings were abandoned and each team could now arrange to meet up whenever the team members wished. If this meant meeting after school, then support staff were paid to attend.

Angella (a part-time Year 5 class teacher and part of the Culture team) noted that there had been a lot of consultation on the new curriculum. She had recently attended with her job-share partner an 'outstanding teacher' course run by the local authority. Each course member had to deliver a five-minute presentation (or mini-lesson) with the other course members playing the role of pupils. Each five minute slot was rigorously timed and then each person received feedback. Angella planned her lesson on developing the skills of 'empathy', with two other course members in a so-called 'triad'. All the mini-lessons were jointly planned within the triad. The context for the learning was the General Election held in May 2010 and so part of the lesson was responding to a photograph of the winner and losers as the results were announced. The course members had to note down how each of the candidates might have felt at that moment.

Natalie (a Year 4 class teacher) had been involved with the 'Every Child a Writer' government-funded programme, which offered additional help to six pupils in Years 3 and 4 who had not made the expected progress with their writing skills. This initiative allowed one-to-one tuition for one hour a week with a tutor for a total of ten hours. The school worked in a cluster of three schools situated in the local area under the guidance of an experienced practising teacher. The tutor was selected to be a teacher from the same school, but not the pupil's class teacher. It was intended that the child would make one sublevel of progress in the ten-week period.

Three areas had been targeted: sentence construction work, phonics and handwriting. The programme had introduced Natalie to new techniques in teaching literacy and had also improved her own levels of differentiation. She commented on the effects of this invention programme both on the pupils and her own professional development:

> It introduced me to new techniques of teaching; it has improved my differentiation from for my pupils; it's given me a lot more confidence. So it's had a huge impact and my class has made fantastic progress this year and whether it's because of that, I don't know … I would say four out of the six have made significant progress in their writing and are now where they should be. Maybe two (less so) who we didn't realise had SEN problems which have only been picked up during this.

The parents were kept fully informed of this process and all had signed a statement saying they supported it. There was some consolidation of the pupils' learning with homework tasks being set on a weekly basis. For one female pupil, it had transformed her attitude in that she had since developed a love for writing that she did not have before.

(ii) Galaxy Primary School

Fiona was the history and RE co-ordinator and Key Stage 2 teacher. She had mentored Steve when he had started working in the school and he had now become the art co-ordinator. They had recently been involved in the 'Power of Reading' project, with the aim of developing more of an enjoyment of reading among pupils. This project is organized by the Centre for Literacy in Primary Education (CLPE). The Centre provided the texts and teaching sequences, as well as useful support from the website. This contained examples of what others had done in the past.

In the opinion of all those interviewed in Galaxy school, the project had a huge impact on literacy and the staff and children had all enjoyed working with the materials. The key element was that the texts themselves were high quality. A Year 5 class was using one of the texts called the 'London Eye Mystery' by Siobhan Dowd and the pupils had to write a letter in the role of one of the characters in the book. Writing structures had helped the pupils improve the quality of their written work. The lesson sequences associated with each book were put together well and could be easily adapted. 'The Highwayman' by Alfred Noyes produced some good artwork and historical ideas from the pupils. They could also contribute to a blog on the CLPE website, including their own views and interpretations of the texts.

Another innovation that had been introduced recently was a 'Documenting' project where Key Stage 2 pupils recorded what was going on in lessons in ways that suited them. Pupils themselves documented how other children learned. They drew pictures or took photographs. It was intended to have the effect of children trying to persuade other pupils that one way of learning might be more effective than another.

The classroom-based staff interviewed had also been involved in a 'Lesson Study' project in Key Stage 2 (DCSF, 2008). They decided what they would like to observe, which reflected an aspect of the curriculum that pupils were struggling with, usually in English (e.g. some aspect of literacy) or maths (e.g. percentages). Each member of staff would work with two others and jointly plan a lesson, which would then be observed. Three pupils would be selected in advance – a more able, middle ability and lower ability child. One member of the group would teach the lesson and the other two staff observed the pupils, to see how they responded. The staff group would meet together after the lesson and share their observations. The three observed pupils were inter-viewed afterwards about how they were answering questions and the extent to which they were paying attention. The pupils did not know they were being observed. A whole day was set aside for this activity and it was perceived as a way of sharing good practice without it being threatening in any way and, at the same time, being excellent profes-sional development.

Karen, the maths co-ordinator and Year 6 teacher, explained that for maths one-to-one tuition was arranged for six pupils in Year 6 who needed additional help. A tutor had come in to help with this work. This initiative, funded by the previous government, had brought in a trained teacher known to the school who did not teach full time but had previously been employed to stretch the gifted and talented pupils in the school. The pupils were withdrawn from the normal class for one hour a week. The learning was focused on the areas of weakness for each pupil, e.g. times tables. It had a very noticeable effect. Karen commented:

I saw significant increases in the children's levels of confidence … I would say that four made a significant improvement and two not so, but that was partly due to their attitude towards it.

The children that participated in that intervention were selected for two reasons: (i) their parents would be supportive; (ii) the children themselves would respond positively.

(iii) Ashacre Primary School

According to Thomas, the headteacher, the two main initiatives the school had been involved with were the Improving Schools Programme (ISP) and the 'Creative Curriculum'.

ISP helped to identify which key skills needed to be improved for each pupil, for example, the use of punctuation in the writing process, or a stronger grasp of the four rules of number. Part of the ISP process was to have 'working walls', which Thomas described in the following way:

> a display will follow the literacy or numeracy unit over two- or three-week period. As the work develops, examples go up on display to remind children of what the process of learning was …. It will have sticky notes on it; bits hanging off and photocopies of children's work that are not double mounted. It means that each classroom has gone from being a beautiful celebratory display to being a display which may look tatty, which one or two staff found very difficult.

The headteacher had decided that all staff would be involved with ISP as the school needed to improve pupils' learning outcomes. It was not decided by popular agreement.

The 'Creative Curriculum' had been introduced as a totally different approach to teaching and learning. It has moved teachers away from reliance on the prescribed QCA schemes of work towards giving pupils the opportunity to decide what they wish to study and think how they may wish to do it. The teacher's role was to negotiate with pupils to 'fit in' different areas of the subject curriculum around the topic being studied. With the 'Creative Curriculum' there had been more collegial discussion about how it might be introduced. It was the less-experienced staff who had struggled to adjust to the changes associated with its introduction. Janet (a Key Stage 1 class teacher) considered that not everything could be shoehorned into a topic within the 'Creative Curriculum'. If a subject like science did not fit in with the topic, then a discrete unit could be taught separately.

Kathleen (a Key Stage 1 class teacher) had been working within the 'Creative Curriculum', which gave more opportunity for the pupils to decide what they wanted to study. It meant that the teacher could only plan one day ahead. The pupils knew they had to cover different areas of learning so the teacher and pupils worked out between them what would happen. This approach to learning had encouraged more creativity and independence. All the pupils had become engaged in working on their own ideas and this had resulted in fewer comparisons being made: i.e. pupils could no longer directly compare their work with the work of others.

The Real Ideas Organization (RIO) had given a sum of money to support the development of a 'Creative Curriculum'. This organization aims to provide financial support for schools to promote change and provide curriculum enrichment opportunities. For example, some of this funding went into helping fund the school's trip to the historic Roman settlement at Caerleon in Newport, South Wales, for those pupils who were from socially disadvantaged backgrounds.

Janet felt that the pupils remembered more easily what they had learned about. When recounting the trip, she would use photos of, for example, the amphitheatre and the barracks to help trigger the pupils' memories of the visit.

Kathleen and Janet taught in Key Stage 1. The most recent initiative they had both been involved with was a storytelling project, where the whole class had learned a story and actions to go with it. This all then fed into their written work and Kathleen was surprised to see how much additional confidence it had given the pupils. She had read the story to the class and then focused on parts, so the pupils learned small sections at a time. Each story lasted a term and contained three-part sentences: 'Early one morning, the farmer woke up and he went out.' A number of time-sequenced words such as 'next' and 'finally' were included and some descriptive language was used as well, to encourage the children to be imaginative by encouraging them to change the story or be a particular character. The effect was to have a wider range of ability of children being able to write in sentences, including the SEN pupils.

Leading The Learning: Teachers' Work with Pupils

(i) Manor Primary School

Angella (a Year 5 class teacher) found it difficult to articulate how she thought she might influence the pupils' attitude to learning. In Years 5 and 6, pupils kept their own learning logs. They reflected on what they had learned and commented on how they felt about their work. They also devised and planned what they might do next.

There was a celebration every week (a so-called Praise Assembly) where teachers nominated pupils for an award that celebrated how they might be addressing their learning difficulties. Angella felt that children were more confident in saying what they could *not* do rather what they could do. Reward cards were also used, which could be stamped when the pupil achieved a specific target.

There was encouragement for pupils to lead their own learning to some extent, by the teacher adapting what they might have in mind to follow the interests of the pupils. A useful starting point was to generate some questions. In literacy lessons, there were two excellent TAs who worked with nine of the lowest-ability pupils in the class. They received additional help while Angella concentrated on the middle- and higher-ability pupils.

There was some focus on the Manor values, as reflected in the 'Skills for Life' mentioned earlier, but as Angella noted:

> to build a culture we have got to be happy with all these words but at the moment we can barely remember them.

Democracy was important in the school in order to allow everyone a voice. Creativity was encouraged. For example, work was done with pupils on a card game called 'My future: My choice'. The game consisted of some existing jobs written on different cards, but some had cards had 'these do not exist yet' written on them. The pupils then had to realize that some jobs in the future would stem from the 'creative industries'.

Natalie (a Year 4 class teacher) was very aware that her pupils learned in different ways so she tried to explain things in a variety of ways. At the start of each topic, she did a mini-assessment to gauge where the pupils were with their learning. In maths, the pupils had a set of 'must' questions, which they all had to attempt before tackling the extension questions.

A good example of helping all the pupils learn effectively was the 'Big Day' in Manor school, held once every term. The 'Culture' team had introduced Spanish into the curriculum, resulting in a 'Big Spain' day. Each teacher ran a 40-minute workshop, which was repeated for all age groups in the school. Each curriculum group was given a 'Big Day' to promote their area of the curriculum. Those pupils with additional learning needs worked in a small group on tasks that would enhance their learning and stretch or challenge them.

(ii) Galaxy Primary School

Karen's main responsibility was teaching maths in Galaxy school to all the pupils in the two classes in Year 6. The main way in which she shared her values with the pupils was by setting clear expectations of what they needed to do in a lesson and how to do it. Karen had been involved in constructing learning ladders based on social rather than academic skills. For example, one ladder on 'collaboration' might have started with the statement: 'I don't listen to what anyone says.' Other areas might include teamwork or questioning skills. This was having an effect, as the pupils knew that they had to work together and that it would not be productive if they were constantly arguing. The pupils were encouraged to listen to each other and take on board what others thought.

Some work had been done with the children on explaining team roles (e.g. chairperson, scribe, envoy, who collects information from other areas). Pupils also now understood more about acting as a team leader and what having to keep other members of the team focused on the task in hand meant.

To ensure that pupils learned effectively, Karen differentiated the lesson so that the learning needs of pupils ranging from level 2 to level 6 were met. The lowest-ability pupils would need examples – a model to work from – and a step-by-step explanation of how to do things. This would also involve support from TAs (either one or two) for two days a week for each class.

On the other three days, Karen worked on her own, so pupils of all abilities had to be given tasks they could get on with independently. They worked in groups, and learning objectives for each group were stated clearly on the board.

Karen used 'talking partners', where an able pupil was paired up with a less-able child. However, there were some disadvantages to this approach, as her comments illustrate:

> children who are more able sometimes find it difficult to communicate their ideas because a lot of the things they can do, they do instinctively.

Group work could also be difficult to organize because the presence of a very dominant pupil may result in other pupils sitting back and engaging in a passive, uncritical form of learning. However, Karen had helped the pupils to understand different roles within group work and thereby improve their teamwork skills. She commented that:

> we've come up with a list of job descriptions so that when children are working in groups they have a title; each of them knows their role within the group and knows what type of characteristics they need to be able to fulfil that role. So you can hear the children talking and saying: 'OK, you can be the scribe because you can write things down quickly; you can be the artist; and you can be the envoy who goes and collects information from other areas.'

Karen periodically used one day to hold a 'maths surgery'. This involved setting the children a task such as:

> creating a book to explain to someone younger how to solve fractions, or creating a board game.

She would write a list of the topics covered in a set period (e.g. a few weeks) and then tell the pupils that they could now see her individually during the 'surgery' lesson to go through a topic that they had not fully understood.

Fiona and Steve, as Key Stage 2 class teachers, encouraged collaboration by arranging for pupils to work in groups of mixed ability and mixed gender. Steve commented that:

> for the majority of pupils, it is difficult sometimes to get everyone fully engaged in that sort of work: some people find it very hard.

Group composition was sometimes determined by the teacher and at other times by the pupils.

In terms of ensuring that all the pupils learned effectively, AfL (especially oral feedback) techniques were used, which helped to direct where the children's learning was going next. They could be aware of what they needed to do to improve. They had personalized targets and could self-check their own progress, which could then be confirmed by the teacher.

In English and maths, six pupils were selected as representative of the whole class (within the Assessing Pupils' Progress [APP] procedures), and their progress was checked very carefully. The evidence was highlighted and photocopied to justify the judgements being made. As there were two Year 5 classes, a total of twelve pupils' work would be assessed across the whole ability range. Their work was stored in folders and was used in moderation exercises.

It was deemed likely that more attention will be paid in the future to addressing the learning needs of increasing numbers of EAL children and those from vulnerable groups to ensure they are making the expected levels of progress.

(iii) Ashacre Primary School

Kathleen and Janet both worked in Key Stage 1. Kathleen felt it was important to be honest with pupils and let them know that she was a learner as well. Janet would communicate with the pupils if they came up with a new piece of information that she was very grateful as such information added to her own knowledge base. She used pretence sometimes when trying to get the pupils to improve an intentionally poorly written piece of work. She would ask the pupils what they thought about the work and how it might be changed to improve its quality. Janet commented on her lead role in establishing good behaviour patterns with the pupils, as an important pre-condition to effective learning. She was very keen on giving the children a choice. If they were being immature, they would receive a warning and suffer the consequences if their behaviour did not improve.

Janet described an interesting example of the ways in which she tried to improve pupils' writing skills following their trip to the Roman settlement in Caerleon, South Wales:

> In literacy, we've been looking at recounts and what [the pupils] need to include, so we used the Caerleon trip as a stimulus for a recount ... They have success criteria in the front of their books ... which say things like to make notes; to write in past tense; use time connectives; add words of interest for the reader.

> *Interviewer*: What's to stop them writing, as they might do at seven years old, We did this; then we did that ...?

> We have modelled and we've talked about time connectives and we've looked at badly written sections where I've put 'and then, and then' and then we talked about it and changed it.

At the start of the summer term, as part of the 'Creative Curriculum', pupils were asked about what topics they might want to cover. The three classes in Years 3 and 4 were all doing different things, but with a strong local interest: one group was researching the coal industry; another was looking at Celtic settlements and their influence on the region before the Romans invaded. The overall theme was 'Under the Ground'. Thomas, the headteacher, noted that:

> some members of staff found it difficult to deal with pupils being so involved in the planning process.

Janet argued that showing respect for the children and giving them consistent messages was important. She pointed out that there were different types of year group. Some did not gel as a team: others really enjoyed working together. She planned very thoroughly and differentiated the work so there was always help available for lower-ability children and extension work for the most able ones.

There was a great deal of liaison with the TAs to make sure they knew what they were doing. The two full-time TAs worked intensively with two statemented SEN pupils. Some of the SEN pupils had moved up one level in reading during the year; i.e. three pupils had moved up from level 1 to level 2. A great deal of effort was made to track the progress of the pupils. In Year 3, National Curriculum levels were not reported to parents, but the tracker information was used to inform their reports.

By using success criteria, the pupils could create a good recount of their learning. The criteria might include items such as: 'make notes; write in the past tense; use time connectives; add words of interest for the reader'.

The use of 'talking partners' (two pupils paired together) was quite effective when the children were sitting on the carpet. However, in larger groups, say of three or four, the pupils could go off task very quickly.

Children were set targets in literacy and numeracy every half term and they were assessed to see if they had managed to achieve their targets. There were problems with this approach, as it had taken a significant amount of time for SEN pupils to make the required progress. These pupils had found it easier to meet their literacy targets compared to their numeracy targets. The literacy targets allowed the pupils to use word banks to write short sentences, but the numeracy targets placed greater reliance on memory, as they included days of the week, months of the year, time etc. This was information they could forget very easily. Less-able pupils struggled with the twelve-hour analogue clock, although full-time TA help had proved very valuable in this respect.

Kathleen used circle time with pupils to:

- build confidence;
- make eye contact;
- listen to others;
- take turns.

The pupils also knew how to use 'carpet time' well – i.e. not to call out. Kathleen commented that:

> if they have done a piece of work they are pleased with, they can sit and read it to the rest of the class.

The pupils knew what their individual targets were and what they had to do to achieve them. They were revised every half term. Examples of graduated targets (of increasing challenge) would be:

- to work with a teacher to make a word bank;
- to work on my own to make a word bank;
- to use a word bank to make my work more interesting.

A word bank would contain words the children might find interesting, listed in alphabetical order. Talking to the pupils was very effective: asking them about what they could remember and what they had learned. In Year 2, starting to use joined-up handwriting did boost their confidence. When it came to developing numeracy skills, the children had improved at explaining how they obtained their answer, rather than simply saying 'I just know it.'

Teacher Collaboration with Other Teachers and Support Staff

(i) Manor Primary School

Angella (as a Year 5 class teacher) worked three days a week and her job share partner worked the other two days. Angella's aptitudes in art and science complemented her partner's skills in literacy and the humanities subjects. Regular phone conversations during the week helped the working relationship to flourish. Angella worked closely with two other Key Stage 2 teachers, who both had their individual teaching styles. She organized the 'Big Draw', which took place once a year. The pupils undertook five workshops, meaning that each teacher would run the same workshop for five different age groups.

Natalie (a Year 4 class teacher and part of the 'Culture' team responsible for RE, art and design and music) referred to the fact that all the lesson planning was displayed in the staff room so that everyone could see what other staff were doing. Collaboration occurred mainly through communication – talking about new initiatives and how to implement ideas. She discussed with other teachers the best ways to work one-to-one with the pupils in the Every Child a Writer initiative. Natalie worked closely with two other teachers in her band (i.e. Years 3 and 4) as they planned all their lessons together, except numeracy. There were regular discussions about how the team was developing the curriculum. With support staff, there was a great deal of discussion about the best ways of helping SEN pupils. Natalie commented that:

> as a recent NQT, it has given me a great opportunity to have my voice heard. In other schools, you are very much at a low level; being involved in the Culture group has given me the opportunity to talk passionately about what I believe in and implement things and influence other people which I would not necessarily have had in other schools.

Perceived barriers to teacher collaboration usually reflected a negative attitude to change; i.e. any proposed initiatives were not needed. Changes to the curriculum could be regarded as implicit criticism of past practice. In addition, there might be some people who cherished their status as a subject co-ordinator and were unwilling to accept changes to their status. If peer observation procedures were introduced to try and stimulate teacher collaboration, then some staff may not be happy with their lessons being observed, which they could associate with judgements being made. If, however, the teacher was going simply to offer an opinion about what went well in the lesson and what had not, that was likely to be more acceptable.

(ii) Galaxy Primary School

Karen (a Year 6 class teacher) worked closely with two other Year 6 teachers (one full time and the other part time). Some of their discussion was based around how different areas of the curriculum were going to be fitted together coherently. For example, the 'Power of Reading' (CLPE) text was set in Brazil, and Karen wanted the children to use their mathematical skills and learn about converting money; i.e. from pounds to the Brazilian currency.

Karen participated in a lesson study (DCSF, 2008) with the other Year 6 teacher. That member of staff taught the lesson while, at the same time, Karen observed particular pupils that she already knew well and their responses to the lesson. This was a very useful professional development tool as a whole day was devoted to this type of lesson study activity and invited the sharing of good practice without it being threatening in any way. Karen noted that:

> NQTs are given time to come and watch my lesson to see how I organize things.

She encouraged other staff to be more adventurous with the development of pupils' mathematical skills. For example, she mentioned she taught a two-week block centred on Physical Education using a context most pupils could enjoy and which was something different. It gave the opportunity for mathematical skills to be developed. She started with the question: 'Does extra PE improve our brain power?' She commented:

> [the pupils] knew that at the end of the two-week block, they had to present all of the data that they had collected, their jumps, their speed, and put it into a graph and present it to the headteacher.

Steve felt that he was very influenced by two other colleagues as well as Fiona (his much more experienced colleague), even though he worked closely with Fiona. The differences in subject-related skills sets that each teacher had were utilized to the full, for the benefit of the pupils.

Collaboration with TAs worked well as the TAs worked with the same children all the time, so knew them well. In addition, they were well qualified and very experienced. The school was used as a location for the display of whole school art projects with local secondary schools. There were a number of special weekly themes that were addressed during the school year (e.g. Money Week; Green Week; Art Week; Science Week). A given member of staff would take responsibility for each week and generate ideas, which could be tried out across the school at a level suitable for the age and abilities of the pupils.

In the headteacher's opinion, time was the main barrier to teacher collaboration. She did not like holding a large number of staff meetings, so they only had one a week. There were more frequent meetings for staff working in specific Key Stages. Fortunately, there were no teachers employed in the school who were engaging in forms of passive resistance to change.

(iii) Ashacre Primary School

Kathleen worked with two other staff members in Years 1 and 2. One of them was an NQT. Mentoring her had involved plenty of discussion and support, as she was dealing with some fairly challenging pupils. Collaboration with other staff involved planning the curriculum, organizing trips and splitting the three classes into teams for sports day. Sharing ideas in areas where the individual teachers acknowledged they had weaknesses themselves was important, e.g. art skills, using ICT etc. The three staff also organized all the necessary resources collectively.

According to Janet (a Year 3 class teacher), work was less collaborative than it used to be when there were two parallel classes in Year 3. Now there were three slightly different year groups: a Year 3 class; a Year 2 class and a mixed Years 2 and 3 class. A great deal of trouble was taken to ensure that there was no repetition across the year groups. Janet felt that this was collaboration at a fairly superficial level. The staff did agree together which area of the 'Creative Curriculum' each would cover. The pupils covered different topics in Year 3 compared to Year 4. Now there was far more collaboration with the TAs.

According to Thomas, the headteacher, one barrier to collaboration was not having parallel classes in a given year group. He argued that teachers did not have as much in common as they might have done with parallel classes. It could be more difficult to have staff free at the same time to do collaborative planning. Internal arrangements in the school allowed staff to be absent from school if they had PPA time, which meant that opportunities to collaborate were more limited.

Some procedures had encouraged collaboration: for example, Foundation Stage profiles were moderated by reception teachers sitting together with Year 1 teachers.

Working in Partnership with Parents

(i) Manor Primary School

Angella (a Year 5 class teacher) discussed the use of texting to provide parents with efficient feedback if they had a query. The same system could be used to send the same message to a whole year group: e.g. 'Swimming kit needed for all Year 5s on Tuesday.'

Trying to get the parents involved in the topics being studied as much as possible had proved effective. In a topic that involved learning about Brazil, Natalie (a Year 4 class teacher) described a project that involved organizing a Manor Primary School carnival (in the style of a Brazilian carnival) where a dance routine was devised and performed by the pupils. The costumes worn in the carnival celebrated the local environment in which the school was situated (e.g. being near a park and a river). It also included carnival food (e.g. jerk chicken and tropical fruit). The pupils were very enthusiastic to tell their parents what they had learned about children living in a capital city such as Rio de Janeiro and what it was like to live in that country.

(ii) Galaxy Primary School

The school has an open-door policy so parents can come and talk about any issue of concern. Karen (maths co-ordinator and Year 6 teacher) was careful about not setting too much homework, as children could get bogged down by it. If the child was involved in receiving additional support through the use of an intervention strategy, this was explained very carefully to the parents. There was a continuous dialogue with parents.

Some parents would have liked more homework, but Karen felt that it should be targeted at meeting the pupils' learning needs and not just be homework for the sake of it. The parents were generally good at letting the teachers know if there was an aspect of English or maths their child was not clear about. With the maths one-to-one tuition programme, the reasons for setting extra homework were explained to the parents.

Fiona (a Key Stage 2 teacher and history and RE co-ordinator) mentioned that contact with parents was on a daily basis, before and after school in the playground. All the subject areas had evenings for parents to encourage learning. Pupils' progress was tracked very carefully.

(iii) Ashacre Primary School

The system whereby children were collected at the end of the day had changed recently. Parents now collected their offspring by hand, which had made it easier for the teacher to say: 'She did a good piece of writing today.' Previously the child would be collected by parents standing well back in the playground. Some parents had found the change difficult to deal with. Others had changed their behaviour and would now come and talk regularly with the class teacher. The emphasis was on making positive comments to parents about their children, especially the SEN pupils.

Janet (a very experienced Year 3 class teacher) knew many of the parents well as she had taught their older children. In her view, trying to help the SEN pupils was difficult because targets were set in meetings with the parents but then often not followed up at home. She commented that:

> I have a tick list for reading so, if the pupils read three times a week, signed by an adult, they have an extra merit for their merit card and that goes towards prizes they try to earn ... It's nearly always the same parents who hear their children read and the same parents who do not hear their children read.

What Does This Evidence Indicate About Teachers Taking Responsibility for Teaching and Learning?

(i) Support for teacher leadership

All the SLTs in the schools visited now delegated more responsibility for teaching and learning than had previously been the case (Harris, 2003). This meant that those experienced staff on higher pay scales (e.g.UPS3) were now expected to be more proactive in their delegated leadership function. For example, Jill (headteacher in Galaxy school) described how relatively inexperienced staff who had been appointed as subject leaders were now being supported by more experienced staff in a mentoring/coaching capacity, acting as a critical friend in the peer review of teaching practice (O'Donoghue and Clarke, 2010).

There was evidence that pupils were involved in the appointment of new staff and made a valuable contribution to Eco-Schools' work.

Support staff were consulted and did participate in decision-making processes to some degree in all the schools visited. In Manor Primary School, TAs had been included in the newly created six areas of learning and they had an equal voice in meetings. For example, the science team contained two staff and three TAs.

(ii) School improvement

There was evidence of more attention being paid to skills development, with strong support for this from the deputy headteacher in Manor primary school (Durrant and Holden, 2006). Curriculum re-organization in the light of the Rose review (DCSF, 2009) had led to six areas of learning being created. Tactical approaches to change were noted by Gray (2005) when specific government funded initiatives were embraced. These focused on providing appropriate interventions aimed at raising underperformance, for example, in maths in Galaxy primary school.

Setting up the Creative Curriculum in Ashacre Primary school certainly appeared to give pupils the chance to show independence in their learning. This was one example of learning becoming more personalized. However, there was evidence of use of target setting on a regular basis as attention was given to raising standards in literacy and numeracy (Dimmock, 2000). One teacher noted the problems of SEN pupils not making the expected progress in a short time period.

(iii) Teachers working with pupils

As regards building a culture of shared values and collaboration with pupils, several teacher-leaders in different schools commented on the importance of circle time to promote respect for the views of other pupils; to build confidence; to learn to take turns; and to help with eye contact. All the teacher-leaders interviewed were keen to listen to learner voice (Durrant and Holden, 2006).

Manor primary school had developed an interesting approach to the life skills the staff wanted the pupils to develop. Pupils devised five levels for each skill in the form of a ladder, with the help of the teacher. For 'collaboration', level 1 might be: 'I do not listen to what anyone else says.' The pupils then self-assessed where they were on the ladder. These statements were displayed on the walls of the classroom and referred to regularly.

Teacher-leaders argued that it was very important to model desired values, such as honesty and respect (Harris and Muijs, 2005). Angella (in Manor primary school) also noted that respect was sometimes spoken about in the context of 'other people's property, space and privacy'. It was also perceived that pupils taking responsibility for their own learning as far as possible was advantageous in helping pupils to become more independent learners.

Other aspects of working with pupils involved, in Manor primary school, use being made of learning logs, which can encourage pupils to develop metacognitive skills (McGregor, 2007) and to be more aware of their own learning (Harris, 2007). Emphasis was placed on differentiation, small-group work (Watkins, 2005) and AfL (Black and Wiliam, 1998). Harris and Muijs (2005) suggested that not all staff would perceive themselves as 'leading the learning' but would feel happier if they were thought of as facilitating the learning. Several schools mentioned the important work of TAs with SEN pupils, especially with helping pupils improve their reading skills (Watkinson, 2003).

(iv) Teachers working collaboratively with other staff

Observation of other teachers at work in the classroom retained its status as being a powerful tool for influencing practice. Formal learning opportunities (Eraut, 2000) arose in Galaxy primary school with the adoption of the lesson study initiative. This was promoted by the headteacher as a good way of sharing best practice.

Joint lesson planning also appeared to be one of the major ways in which teachers collaborated in their work. However, in Ashacre primary school there was less collaboration than in the past because classes were now of mixed ages rather than parallel.

(v) Teachers working with parents

The main aspects centred around effective communication between parents and teachers. The schools visited all had an open-door policy so that parents could ask questions or express any concerns. Parents were kept well informed when targeted intervention strategies were devised for their children. One teacher in Ashacre primary school did note the difficulties of persuading parents to read with their children at home.

8 Leading the Learning in Primary Schools in Wales

Distributed Leadership: SLT Perspectives

(i) Green Primary School

Gaynor, the headteacher, felt that team leaders needed to be given responsibility for various aspects of school improvement to generate improved outcomes for learners. This was seen to be a nurturing process, as teachers could then be encouraged to become future school leaders. Her role was one of supporting a member of staff as he or she exercised that responsibility without the need to be constantly looking over his or her shoulder, wondering what the headteacher was thinking. There were no barriers, as different people could exercise leadership in different ways. The review of the staffing structure was an example of involvement in decision-making where two recent extensive consultations with staff had occurred that were seen to be an important part of the process. Support teachers worked closely with classroom teachers and contributed to decision-making at team meetings based on Key Stages.

(ii) Central Primary School

According to Christine, the assistant headteacher, staff were kept well informed even though all the major decisions were made by the head and governors. Classroom teachers were invited to SLT meetings if there were items of interest to them under discussion. Regular staff meetings were held weekly and were attended by all members of staff, including TAs and students. Currently, all staff were working on new schemes of work. The school council was perceived to be a useful body to allow 'pupil voice'. For example, following a debate in the school council, money was raised for much-needed playtime equipment.

Pupils were now being given more curriculum choice through a 'Continuous Provision' programme, in response to the introduction of a more skills-based approach to learning in Wales in 2008. The 'Continuous Provision' programme was an attempt to move away from a subject-dominated curriculum towards a theme-based cross-curricular model.

It operated in Key Stage 2 (i.e. pupils aged between 7 and 11 years old). There were five learning areas, each of which generated an activity that was followed during the week. These areas included 'Data Den', a maths investigation; 'Creative Corner', which was music or art based; design technology and construction; a 'Writers Workshop'; and the 'Investigation' area, which was science based.

The activities were carefully differentiated to suit all ability levels. If children who needed additional linguistic support worked on an activity, then a bi-lingual support teacher would be available to them.

Pupils had to cover all five areas, but they were able to choose what they would like to do. They worked through an activity and then filled in a passport in which they evaluated their own learning. The staff signed the passports when they were completed. This had required a lot of planning. Christine commented:

> what is interesting is that the children have really enjoyed their learning. They are going home and speaking to their parents about what they have learned in school …

Year 6 pupils had given a presentation to the governors explaining how much their learning had changed and how they were now enjoying learning more than previously.

(iii) Avenue Primary School

Sally discussed the idea of distributed leadership from more of a hierarchical perspective in relation to a distribution of responsibilities. She felt that the teachers were expected to lead the learning in their classrooms. The class teachers oversaw the work of their TAs.

Staff participation in decision-making took various forms: for example, being consulted in staff meetings; making use of working parties to come up with suggestions for an aspect of school improvement to be presented to the whole staff; using performance management strategies; holding weekly planning meetings between class teachers and TAs; discussing classroom-based behaviour management policies, which were decided by the pupils themselves; having an eco-council and a school council, which both contained elected pupil representatives.

The pupils also had some input into deciding what they might learn and how they might learn something, within a teacher-guided framework. The teachers generated the themes to be investigated.

(iv) Bridge Primary School

Sheila, the headteacher, referred to the help she received from a very experienced SLT (known as the Leadership and Support Team). This met fortnightly to help debate and then decide on the strategic direction of the school. Two senior staff had been given the responsibility of introducing the development of the International Primary Curriculum (IPC) (see the next section for more details).

Each year group consisted of two classes, so one member of staff was designated as the group leader for that year group. Support staff were able to take a leading role in developing first aid procedures or promoting health and safety issues.

Bridge school had a three-year rolling programme of school self-evaluation and all the key stakeholders were consulted on a regular basis. For example, support staff might be surveyed in the autumn term, and the pupils would then be given a questionnaire in the following spring term.

School Improvement: Recent Involvement in Educational Initiatives

(i) Green Primary School

Gillian, school improvement leader for Key Stage 2, thought that designing a new curriculum in Key Stage 2 to fit in the key skills was a real challenge. She was responsible for standards of numeracy and teaching of maths throughout the school. She was the school's improvement leader in Key Stage 2 and had been teaching the Years 3 and 4 curriculum for about eleven years. The school ran the 'Springboard' programme, which targeted pupils who were not making as much progress as they should be in maths. They received additional help, half an hour twice a week as a small group. This consisted of an intensive coaching session run by an experienced TA and had been running for the last couple of years.

Jane, Early Years and Key Stage 1 team leader, noted that the main initiative at the present time was concerned with trying to establish firmly the Foundation Phase, which was currently statutory for children in nursery and reception. One of the current aims was to set up a multi-sensory environment as an area of learning, which included outdoor education. The children would be challenged to learn by using water, mud, sand etc. This had led to some interesting learning approaches being developed: for example, with a theme like 'The Seaside', pupils might think about how they might remove sand from their drink or build a castle so that it had water around it as a moat.

Jane discussed some of difficulties associated with a theme-based approach to learning:

> Because we are working on a themed approach, you may not necessarily cover every subject, but during their time with you, they have covered everything.

> *Interviewer*: How do you try and avoid 'black holes' appearing in their experience?

That's careful planning; it is looking carefully at what is happening in the nursery and in reception and areas of development throughout. It is human nature – every teacher covers what they like to do. It is my job as the team leader to identify what has not been done that needs to be done and when can it be done? How can you progress from looking at water in reception and what are they doing with water in Year 2?

Here, the emphasis on learning was the development of skills, whilst at the same time giving due recognition to the demands of the various subject areas in each of the contexts that can be addressed, as the Foundation Phase develops over time.

(ii) Bridge Primary School

The school had adopted the IPC in the last three years, which had given staff the opportunity to bring in a more thematic approach in line with the Skills Framework (DCELLS, 2008b), as advocated by the Welsh Assembly Government (WAG). This had provided the chance to move away from a more subject-based curriculum, which was previously taught in discrete time slots. It had also created more opportunities for personalization of learning and introduced pupils to more of an international dimension to their learning. Its introduction had not been without its problems because the more traditional subject-based co-ordinators were concerned about a loss of subject-based status with the move towards a more skills-based curriculum. In the headteacher's (Sheila's) view, it did help that a recent Estyn inspection indicated that the school was highly successful.

The IPC allowed pupils to have more of a 'voice', as the pupils could choose to focus on a 'host' country as well as making comparisons with their own home country, Wales. So, for example, if the topic under discussion was concern about the disappearing rainforest, then the host country would be Brazil. The pupils could decide what they wanted to investigate and how they might go about it.

According to Sheila, staff in the school were very proactive in coming up with ideas. One had suggested organizing a community after-school event that could raise funds for a PA system for the school. This would involve musicians and choirs and raise the profile of music among the local community.

The local authority had advocated the use of Building Learning Power (BLP) (Claxton, 2002) with pupils in recent times. Teachers therefore focused on helping the pupils learn more about learning itself, particularly in terms of developing resilience and teaching them what it means. The chief aim of BLP was to raise children's levels of independence, so that if they did not know how to progress, they could then follow a pattern that would help them to start to progress. For example, Sheila commented:

Five or six years ago, children would put up their hand and say 'I'm stuck, Sir/Miss. I can't do it.' Now, by the time the children get to Year 6, they think: 'Can I go on the Internet and get the answer? Can I ask my friend? Have I looked something up in a book?'

The introduction of the IPC has had a big impact on Year 6 pupils by giving them more opportunities to be creative and independent and allowing them to make more choices. IPC had allowed more flexibility in how the curriculum was being delivered, because it was now much more skills based. The drawback, according to John (team leader for Key Stage 2), was some concerns about areas of the curriculum that were not being tackled. These would be the Foundation subjects, as the Core subjects like maths and English were being covered in a more discrete fashion. Similarly, science, ICT, RE and Welsh were areas of the curriculum that were being covered as separate subjects. This reflected a concern that it would not be desirable for Year 6 pupils to leave the school with some areas of the curriculum having been neglected.

Both Year 6 teachers interviewed had been heavily involved in the introduction of IPC. Each unit of work lasted about half a term and it had been extensively evaluated: what had worked well; what could be improved upon? David (science co-ordinator and member of the schools' SLT) noted the initial difficulties, two years previously, that were experienced when trying to fit together or match a skills-based scheme such as IPC with the local authority-inspired science scheme.

John was involved in a partnership project with another school located in a different area of the city that did not have the same social mix of pupils as Bridge Primary School. A pastoral programme was organized and its aim was to teach Key Stage 2 children more about mixing/socializing with pupils of the same age from different cultural backgrounds. This was intended to prepare pupils for the transition to secondary school.

(iii) Central Primary School

Ken (as Key Stage 2 team leader) discussed his involvement with 'Continuous Provision', which promoted more of a child-led approach to learning. This occupied approximately eight hours of learning each week. If a given area was over-subscribed (i.e. had more than twelve children) they were asked to choose another area. The biggest challenge with this approach was ensuring that all the resources were available for the pupils. With 'Continuous Provision', staff resources were an issue, because ideally each of the five areas should have a support teacher attached, but that was only possible in three of the areas.

Various examples were quoted, including designing a fairground in the 'Creative Corner' and designing new buildings for a recently renovated local docklands area. Ken commented that the degree of independence exhibited by the pupils had grown over the school year. It was argued that employing a 'Continuous Provision' approach had encouraged the development of thinking skills and resulted in a change to the teacher's role to that of being a facilitator of learning.

There was some initial stimulus material provided by the teacher when introducing the theme of the week, which provided the context in which the learning was situated, as well as some background knowledge for pupils. In each of the five areas, there were skills-based challenges for pupils to tackle.

Lesley, a Year 5 class teacher, was involved in developing a 'Healthy School' initiative: i.e. healthy lunchboxes; more exercise; walking to school etc. She was also the teacher representative on the school's eco committee and worked with the class representatives. The school was working towards the 'Green Flag' award, which, if successful, would designate the school as being both environmentally friendly and sustainable. Lesley considered that such activities contributed to the skills-base of every child. She commented that:

> sometimes children who find it hard to concentrate in a classroom setting take on a much more active role.

For example, the pupils could play an active role in the school's co-operative, which sold fruit and vegetables to the parents. The children involved (who were in Years 4 and 5) did all the marketing and advertising; sourced the produce; kept records of stock etc. The pupils would get the orders ready and met their parents at the end of the school day, who then collected their orders.

(iv) Avenue Primary School

Apart from WAG-driven initiatives, staff in Avenue Primary school could come up with their own ideas. Two years ago, the newly appointed literacy co-ordinator realized that an overhaul of current practice in relation to literacy and phonics was needed. This teacher had seen some good practice and she thought it was a good idea. In a staff meeting she described the materials and results and then suggested a training date to provide more information. It was trialled in the school so that teachers could see its effects for themselves.

Ann had responsibility for implementing the skills curriculum across Key Stage 2. It was also the first year of setting up the IPC in the school, in a very similar fashion to IPC in Bridge Primary school. This placed a greater emphasis on learning goals, which were largely determined by the pupils. They could work at their own level and be successful. Ann used post-it notes, which the pupils completed, containing details of things they would like to find out about.

Laura was involved in setting up the Foundation Phase curriculum in the reception class, which would roll over into Year 1. She was also involved with another initiative called 'Stay and Play', which encouraged parents to come into the classroom to help them understand more about the curriculum and to be more involved in their child's education. She worked with a group of Foundation Phase pupils who were targeted for help with language. This involved using a systematic phonics programme called 'Read Write Inc' developed by Ruth Miskin. A speech and language therapist led the programme in the school and it was targeted on improving reading, comprehension, spelling and writing.

Leading The Learning: Teachers' Work with Pupils in The Classroom

(i) Green Primary School

Teachers were working with pupils to set their own learning goals, especially in the Foundation Phase. Gaynor, as the headteacher, was very keen on pupils acquiring skills in literacy and numeracy. She argued that if you want to develop the skills of enquiry, for example, and the pupils had not got the necessary literacy skills, then they could not carry out any form of enquiry effectively. Giving pupils the opportunity to plan and direct their own learning allowed them to think for themselves, with the teacher being more of a facilitator of learning. Allowing children to set their own targets and using AfL techniques helped the learning process. The primary focus in the last three years had been to improve the standards of reading, helping children to become more functional readers. It was now possible for the least able who needed additional support to be taught in smaller groups.

Gillian (school improvement leader for Key Stage 2) argued that she organized the pupils' work and also that of the support staff. In relation to building a culture of shared values, Gillian felt that pupils needed to see respect being given to co-workers in the classroom and around the school. It was important to admit to making mistakes openly in front of the whole class and being honest about her own feelings when it was appropriate.

For Gillian, as a Key Stage 2 teacher, the ability to differentiate was seen as crucial. Three levels of planning were required as a minimum when planning lessons, which were targeted at pupils who were achieving at different levels. Giving the pupils work they could be successful with helped and frequent monitoring of their work meant that a 'finger could be kept on the pulse' with their learning. Having a TA who may be strategically seated next to a SEN pupil and very near to a few pupils who might need some extra support was very helpful in terms of their learning.

Some pupils did not seem to realize that what they might have just stated orally could form the basis of what they might write down. The TA would also encourage the pupils to write down their ideas, build their confidence and reassure them.

Occasional field trips were also useful in bringing the learning 'alive'. As part of a Welsh history topic on the Celts, Year 3 and 4 pupils had recently visited the site of an original Celtic fort in Pembrokeshire. Some Celtic roundhouses have been built on the site and the pupils dressed up as Celts for the day.

Jane (Early Years and Key Stage 1 team leader) considered that she led by example and gave clear guidance, making sure the support staff were clear about what was expected of them. It was important to allow younger children to be active learners whilst at the same time controlling the amount of independence they actually have. To build a culture of shared values, Jane felt that modelling how to behave was influential, as was not being afraid to admit that she did not know everything. She was very keen the pupils learned not to shout over each other or take over (i.e. dominate) a group activity.

In the Foundation Phase, when pupils were reading text out loud, the TA helped individuals who were having difficulties with speaking their high-frequency words. It was necessary to stretch and challenge the most able pupils, especially in maths, where they might do some problem solving activities. In Technology, they might have to build a free-standing bridge over water using Lego, straws etc. Such challenge was needed because these pupils could become complacent if there was a lack of challenge in the activities tackled.

The subject-based curriculum was still there to some degree, as in the Foundation Phase there were areas of learning. But children's progression in terms of learning was described as being in stages, not ages. This was one of the justifications for mixed-age classes.

(ii) Bridge Primary School

Sheila (the headteacher) described how Year 6 pupils had the opportunity to lead the learning of Year 1 pupils. This was seen as adding to the existing buddy relationships between Year 1 and 6. Year 1 did a project called 'Going on Holiday' where the holiday itself was set in Greece. She noted that:

> The Year 6s set up one hall as a mock airport. They had passport control; a check-in desk; a waiting area; sweets and newspapers. The pupils then went into the next hall where the chairs were laid out as in an aeroplane. The pilot and cabin crew were all there and the Year 1s dressed up for their holiday wearing jazzy sunglasses, flowery shirts, carrying a suitcase and their passports.

For pupils, leading their own learning was a high priority. Involving them in setting their own targets was seen to be a crucial part of the learning process. In addition, a further change to be introduced in the future was for IEPs to be written in more child-friendly language. The SEN pupil would work together with the teacher to write these.

First and foremost, the most fundamental cultural imperative in the school was inclusion. Generating a sense of belonging for all pupils and their parents then meant that the staff could have high expectations of the pupils and behavioural policies were applied consistently across the school. This approach was summarized in the school mission statement as 'Learning and living in harmony', which had been agreed by all the stakeholders in the school.

For John (team leader for Key Stage 2, working with Year 6 pupils), it was important to make a good start at the beginning of the school year to help pupils learn effectively. He described this process in the following way:

> I'll sit down with the Year 5 teachers and we'll have a discussion on each pupil. We'll have a look at their targets and their teacher assessments. We'll have a look at their predictions as well. The teachers will also get them to do a bit of writing for me, so when they first come into my class and sit down, I'll have this piece of writing in front of me, which does tell you a lot about a child.

There was some differentiation in maths so that the more able worked together and those pupils who needed extra support would receive this from teachers or EAL staff. Some pupils might have good mathematical understanding but not the language with which to express that ability orally or in writing.

John used the WALT (We Are Learning Today) and WILF (What I am Looking For) objectives system to help with self- and peer assessment. Success criteria (in effect the WILF) were also stressed as being important and these were discussed with the pupils.

In John's view, Bridge school was a very inclusive school that celebrated all the major religious festivals such as Christmas, Eid, Ramadan etc. He allowed choices to be made in relation to learning. These included: what the pupils wanted to do; how they wanted to do it; what they wanted to do next.

An example of very successful integration was given as a female pupil from Africa who had arrived in Bridge Primary school having experienced and witnessed some horrific scenes. At first, she was both aggressive and frightened. She was buddied up with one of the female indigenous pupils and her language skills developed rapidly. This girl had tremendous support from her family and she made rapid progress in the relatively short time that she was in the school, leaving as a level-five pupil.

John did not feel comfortable with the label of 'classroom leader' but he did consider himself to be a facilitator of learning. However, on occasions he would, especially in a subject like maths, lead from the front and explain how to work a problem out with the whole class. He also accepted that he was a role model for the pupils, both in terms of attitudes to learning and modelling good behaviour.

David (science co-ordinator and member of the SLT) felt that differentiating the planned teaching approaches to be used in lessons was vital. He was able to call upon the services of a part-time teaching assistant to help small groups with numeracy or literacy difficulties.

David used an effective technique that he referred to as 'closing the gap' marking (DfES, 2007), which his school had been using in recent years. It took the form of posing a question or questions at the end of a piece of pupil's written work, which might help to move the pupil on in terms of understanding of a topic. He illustrated this technique in the following way:

> You've done this piece of writing about 'A day in the life of a blood cell': can we take it further with a question that I write at the end of the work? For example, what is the name of the essential thing in the air in order to be able to stay alive? The child will answer it and you often get a nice dialogue going at the end of a piece of writing between the teacher and the child.

Alternatively, questions might be asked, such as: 'Did you enjoy that topic? If so, why? What could be done differently to help you learn more effectively?'

It was very useful for pupils to witness desirable behaviour when staff discussed things with each other. Both David and John agreed that they engaged in learning themselves and were willing to talk about what they had learned with the pupils.

(iii) Central Primary School

According to Christine, the assistant headteacher, at the beginning of term pupils were told about a topic they were going to study based on the Celts and Romans. They were asked about what they would like to learn about, which gave them an opportunity to lead their own learning. Pupils often did class assemblies for their parents and they were asked to write their own scripts. They contributed their own research, shared their ideas and, if they were good, they could be incorporated into the assembly.

Christine emphasized the inclusive ethos of the school by way of an example and described International Day, where the children wore their national costumes to demonstrate their pride in their origins.

In the context of the class teacher learning the learning, this was about managing the other adults who were in the classroom. The school had Ethnic Minority Language and Achievement Service (EMLAS) teachers (i.e. qualified EAL teachers who came in to work with pupils whose second language was English). Ken (Year 5 and 6 team leader) felt that one thing that needed to be addressed was the removal of duplication of work: i.e. avoiding having two adults doing the same thing. A bilingual support teacher was also available to help pupils understand what might be said in a video. In Ken's view, it was most important that the teacher led by example. That meant role modelling desirable behaviour in front of children, for example by showing respect to opinions of others. There was another crucial element to leading in the classroom, which was being willing to admit that as a learner oneself the teacher did not always know the answer when a pupil asked a question. This could then lead to a teacher response: 'How can we find out? Use the Internet; discuss it with the rest of my group etc.' Giving children greater independence in their own learning had motivated them.

To build a culture of shared values, promoting challenge in the pupils' learning was important. Ken was continually trying to help them ask better questions in response to their curiosity about a topic. Bilingual staff helped pupils with cultural interpretation. A child from one culture might say something to another pupil from a different culture that could be unintentionally offensive. Lesley discussed the importance of the International Day to the children, as noted by Christine earlier.

To ensure that pupils learned effectively, regular assessments were used throughout the school year, which helped to track their progress. All work was suitably differentiated, which, due to the multi-ethnic backgrounds of the pupils, was a key issue. Every half term work was assessed and then stored as evidence in a portfolio, particularly in English and maths. Speaking and listening skills could be recorded on CD. Regular efforts were made to boost the pupils' reading ages, so some targeted children did not attend assembly for two mornings a week and instead had additional reading support sessions.

Building positive attitudes to learning was founded on developing effective relationships with pupils. This entailed sharing with them immediately they walked through the classroom door, through the use of informal chat. The teacher being available to speak and listen to them was seen as vital in building these relationships. Collaboration was encouraged through the extensive use of group work. Frequently moving around from one group to another helped to keep the pupils on task and also assisted them in thinking through ideas.

From Lesley's perspective as a class teacher, working effectively with pupils in the classroom was the result of a whole school approach to building collaboration with the pupils, which recognized their very diverse backgrounds. She felt they were 'submerged in a culture of acceptance'. All the major religious festivals were celebrated and each year the school put on an international day where pupils could dress up in their national costume. They also sang songs and performed dances that reflected their ethnic origins.

Lesley gave an example related to exploiting pupils' curiosity about a wide range of topics in the following way, which demonstrated how she handled the situation:

> I had a particularly inquisitive class last year with a hunger for learning. You would be halfway through a maths lesson and they would come up with completely random questions which were science related and came from nowhere. Rather than hamper that inspiration, I would say to them, 'Right, ten minutes at the end of every day, you can ask me absolutely anything you want. It doesn't matter what it's about.'

(iv) Avenue Primary School

Sally, from an SLT perspective, commented that the pupils always had targets, and when they were achieved there would be a discussion with the child about something that he or she needed to improve upon. With older pupils, they could begin do some peer assessment. Such a process required the pupils to be trained to be tactful and to become skilful in feeding back to one of their peers.

Sally noted that some boys in the Foundation Phase would 'pedal on a bike all day for a week'. The idea then was to give the pupils some ownership of what they did and how they did it without giving them the complete liberty to do whatever they wanted – i.e. guided choice.

Sally felt that the Christian ethos of the school was 'stamped' on everything the school did. To build the culture of shared values, a great deal of emphasis was placed on circle time to promote listening to other people's opinions, promote respect etc.

According to Laura, who worked with children in the Foundation Phase (FP), leading the learning involved modelling activities for the benefit of new staff or trainee teachers as well as directing them when necessary. An emphasis on the use of open-ended questioning was very important, as some staff tended to ask closed questions rather than draw out the pupils' thinking skills. Laura relied on feedback from support staff, such as an experienced nursery nurse who could be trusted to work in whatever way she considered appropriate. The nursery nurse commented that she:

> did not feel undermined if somebody [i.e. another member of the team] wanted to teach something in a different way.

Ann (as team leader for Key Stage 2) thought her classroom was 'driven by pupil voice', which meant listening to what the pupils wanted to do. She considered that she was leading by providing the scaffolding for the pupils' learning. She tried to help pupils learn effectively by trying to differentiate all tasks appropriately and by taking account of the pupils' learning style. The less-able pupils needed shorter, less-challenging tasks. Ann aimed to ensure that there was a range of learning strategies available for pupils to adopt. In practice, the pupils chose what they wanted to do and how they were going to do it. As an example of differentiation, in maths:

> some pupils just want to answer written questions; some pupils want to produce something visual like a poster …

The key according to Laura (as team leader for the Foundation Phase) was observation of pupils in their current learning situations and careful planning to develop the skills included in the Skills Framework (DCELLS, 2008b). It was also being aware of what the pupils needed to do next through close collaboration with all the relevant staff and careful record keeping.

Laura was a very experienced teacher and had a good grasp of child development in Early Years education. She noted that in Wales there was a child profile guidance document (DCELLS, 2009), which contained all the aspects of skill development. The nursery class had one member of staff to eight children for a term, so that member of staff could get to know those pupils well. There was a wide range of ability in the nursery, so differentiation was very important, in order to plan activities and interventions to move the learning of all pupils forward. Targeting maths (e.g. numeracy skills) or listening skills was particularly relevant for this age group. Some pupils knew their numbers from one to twelve and others might have no knowledge at all of number sequences.

Teacher Collaboration with Other Teachers and Support Staff

(i) Green Primary School

Gillian (school improvement leader for Key Stage 2) worked closely with five staff (two full-time and one part-time teacher and two TAs). This was a new team that had only been together for nine months. A good rapport had been built up in a relatively short time and, where there were disagreements, the staff would agree to differ. Status and seniority did come to the fore when it came to making the final decision about something because Gillian was the senior member of staff among the colleagues with whom she worked closely.

Jane, working in the Foundation Phase (FP), argued that collaboration with other staff was about being open and allowing other staff to voice their views. She worked with seven other staff and there were no hidden agendas. She commented that 'everyone helped everyone else out'.

The headteacher (Gaynor) noted that the lack of finance was possibly one of the biggest barriers to teacher collaboration. Arranging PPA so that teams could work together had become very difficult. Giving staff additional time during the day to work on projects together would be ideal, but it was expensive to provide cover for staff to be released.

(ii) Bridge Primary School

One area in which John (team leader for Key Stage 2) considered that he collaborated closely with three other staff (one support teacher and two teachers) was in relation to the scrutiny of data, looking for evidence of under-achievement. The ensuing discussion would then focus on devising strategies to help particular pupils to improve. David felt in his role as science co-ordinator that he was regularly passing on resources and ideas from the local authority advisers to staff in school.

The headteacher (Sheila) considered time would be an obvious barrier to collaboration. Occasionally, there might be a clash of personalities within a year group where anything more than superficial collaboration could be problematic.

(iii) Central Primary School

Ken argued that establishing positive relationships with all the staff was an important aspect of collaboration. He had run in-service training courses in school and in the local authority on the use of ICT. Such training was presented at different levels, meaning it was accessible for everyone. One issue that had arisen recently was that TAs needed further training if they were to support the pupils' learning effectively. The TAs did not always fully understand how best to use ICT software. A step-by-step guide was produced to show each step on the screen; for example, to show how one might add a box around some text or a diagram. It had helped to boost their confidence. It also included the use of Publisher, which was better than just using Word alone, because in Publisher it was easier to drag a text box around on the screen.

The Assistant headteacher, Christine, felt that there were no major barriers to various forms of teacher collaboration. There were regular staff meetings, year group meetings and the curriculum planning was done collaboratively, which was particularly beneficial for inexperienced teachers and NQTs. Support staff also attended these meetings. The quality of collaboration was enhanced because of the joint planning arrangements in the school. For example, Years 3 and 4 met up on a Friday afternoon while the children followed a two part-curriculum involving (i) sport and (ii) other designated activities set in advance by the teacher, which were supervised by a TA. The sport was taken by a private organization who provided the coaches, which the school paid for. The coaches took various sporting activities with the pupils in the yard.

During the planning time, all the work was downloaded on to the school's server and included short-term, medium-term and longer-term planning.

(iv) Avenue Primary School

Laura worked closely with three full-time staff (i.e. the Year 6 teacher and the link teachers in Years 2 and 3) and seven others (mainly TAs) and met up regularly (once a week after school) with reception and nursery staff to plan the ongoing development of the Foundation phase. She noted that:

> TAs now have to do a lot more work, particularly in relation to assessment and record keeping. Planning is now done in a far more collaborative manner than in the past. A post-it note system is used to pinpoint where the learning needs to go next. This forms part of their profile and these notes are discussed at regular intervals with the relevant staff.

Laura worked with other staff to scrutinize standards of literacy across the school and provide feedback to colleagues. It was not easy to communicate with a colleague to say that, as a result of the monitoring process, the expectations for a pupil or pupils were not high enough. Sometimes, staff needed some help in understanding more about what might be an appropriate set of expectations for pupils at level 3 or 4 or 5 etc.

What had been effective was aligning the work of parallel staff in the same year group. Avenue Primary school had received praise from Estyn on their teamwork but it had taken a great deal of effort to troubleshoot any apparent differences between teachers. This takes account of the fact that parents were quick to spot weaknesses and differences in educational experiences of pupils in parallel year groups.

Sally, as a member of the SLT, noted that there were always going to be different approaches to teaching pupils. Effective teacher collaboration assumed that staff were placed with those adults with whom they worked well. There was a ratio of one adult to eight pupils in reception and there were three higher-level qualified TAs. All of this (i.e. the size of teams of staff working together) had to be managed by the TLR post-holder. Much of the collaboration took place after school as there was no funding for colleagues to meet up during the day.

One potential barrier to teacher collaboration was that it could be difficult collaborating with a partner who did not share the same work ethic. This might result in an uneven amount of work being put in by one colleague in comparison to another.

Working in Partnership with Parents

(i) Green Primary School

Use was made of home reading record books, which the parents could write in if they had listened to their child read. These were checked once a week and the teacher fed back appropriate comments to the parents. Spelling sheets were also used, which the parents could become involved with. Rather than just learning the words, the pupils had a worksheet with puzzles and quizzes based on these words, which was sent home for the parents to see. Stickers were also used to celebrate achievement (e.g. going up a level in literacy). Parents sometimes came in as a volunteer to listen to a group of pupils read.

(ii) Bridge Primary School

John, as team leader for Key Stage 2, had the advantage of being a long-serving member of staff. He commented on the importance of direct phone contact with the parents of a pupil who was not achieving his or her potential. The ensuing discussion may help to reveal any underlying problems and may also suggest remedies to help that pupil get back on track. He mentioned a useful routine in the school wherein they held celebration assemblies every Friday and pupils were presented with certificates for something excellent that they had done.

(iii) Avenue Primary School

According to Laura, who taught in a nursery, there was an open-door policy for parents to come in and ask questions at any time. The focus was mainly on the child's learning, usually reading books. However, another focus could be pressure for homework, even when it may not be appropriate for children aged four or five years old. Laura had held a phonics workshop for parents recently to explain what the school was doing to help with reading. She considered that the parents seemed to think that the learning going on in school was far more important than the learning being done at home. The nursery and reception years were very important for building positive teacher–parent relationships.

What Does This Evidence Indicate About Teachers Taking Responsibility for Teaching and Learning?

(i) Support for teacher leadership

An example of this was shown by the headteacher, Gaynor, in Green school, who felt it was important for team leaders to have responsibility for school improvement (Harris, 2003). There was general support for the notion of teacher leadership (Durrant and Holden, 2006) although it was evident that formal delegation through TLR post-holders indicated a pre-eminence of the hierarchical organizational structure (Busher, 2006). The idea of pupils leading their own learning was supported in terms of allowing choice and developing pupils' ownership of their work. However, it was recognized that ongoing concerted efforts needed to be made to raise pupils' standards of literacy and numeracy in Wales.

(ii) School improvement

Most of the responses here were focused on the implementation of the 'Skills curriculum' (DCELLS, 2008b) and the Foundation Phase arrangements (DCELLS, 2008c). A number of the teacher-leaders highlighted the switch from a subject-based approach to a more thematic approach. This tended to dominate the discourse, as these changes were still being worked through and were quite a radical departure from previous practice. One teacher-leader noted the positive influence of Claxton's (2002) 'Building Learning Power' approach to learning, which was focused on developing more independent learners.

(iii) Teachers working with pupils

As regards building a culture of shared values and collaboration with pupils, it is accepted that the perspectives offered by teacher-leaders are formulated around the notion of their work-related identities and that the values they espouse act 'as filters that shape the processes of teaching, learning and decision-making' (Busher, 2006, p. 80).

Teachers were able to identify a number of values that pupils could learn through observing them in action. Respect was modelled by teachers in various ways and the use of circle time was advocated as a means by which respect for the views of other pupils could be promoted. In several of the schools visited, inclusion and acceptance of pupils from many different ethnic backgrounds were high priorities and there were opportunities for pupils to express their own cultural heritage (e.g. International Day in Central primary school). It was evident that the teachers were more than willing to be open and honest about their own strengths and weaknesses with the pupils they taught; i.e. the notion of teachers as learners (Durrant and Holden, 2006). Several staff mentioned the necessity for there being sufficient challenge in the tasks pupils tackled and for clear expectations to be communicated to pupils about their learning.

Other aspects of working with pupils included differentiation being important for staff as well as setting an appropriate level of challenge. This could be interpreted as pupils working in their ZPD (Vygotsky, 1978). The positive benefits of using various AfL techniques were noted by several teacher-leaders. In Bridge primary school, where the prevailing culture was one of acceptance and inclusion and setting high expectations was felt to be important. The teacher-leaders were generally very keen on the idea of pupils taking responsibility for their own learning (Harris, 2007). Targeted interventions were used as necessary.

(iv) Teachers working collaboratively with other staff

There was plenty of evidence of collaboration with colleagues (Durrant and Holden, 2006). A teamwork ethic (Harris, 2003) was noticeable in relation to the frequent discussions or meetings held, which were mainly concerned with planning the curriculum. In Central school, more formal organized collaboration events (Eraut, 2000) took place one afternoon a week. Bearing in mind the difficulties in using level descriptors, which are based on skills, it was not surprising that internal moderation of work in a Key Stage had helped to generate a clearer understanding of what constituted work at level 3 or level 4. Strategic use was made of TAs to help develop literacy skills (Watkinson, 2003).

The barriers to teacher collaboration included a lack of time for teachers to meet together and a lack of finance for cover, as teachers' PPA time rarely coincided.

(v) Teachers working with parents

Here, several schools mentioned the value they placed on the celebration of achievement. Again, they had open-door policies towards parents, who could ask questions or express their concerns. One aspect mentioned was the development of literacy skills, but one teacher-leader provided an interesting insight: parents seemed to believe that learning done in school was more important than learning done at home.

9 Leading the Learning in Secondary Schools in England

Distributed Leadership: SLT Perspectives

(i) Quarry Secondary School

Michael, the deputy headteacher, felt that leadership was distributed throughout the school and staff were empowered to do their work. However, there were clear boundaries and he commented that:

> We [as the SLT] set parameters and constraints that we expect staff to operate in and there is a very rigorous quality assurance system.

Michael admitted that more could be done to allow staff to take justifiable risks and learn from them. In his view, Quarry school did have an ethos of continuous improvement and a willingness to be self-critical. He made an insightful comment concerning changes in the school:

> It is for the SLT to empower individuals and allow them to take a risk, knowing that sometimes the project they want to pursue may not work.

Such a scenario may well mean that those individuals will learn from their inability to succeed and be better placed to be more successful in the future.

The SLT met with team leaders of the support staff once every half term in order to discuss developments on a local and national scale, as well as the key issue of helping to raise the standards of teaching and learning. As far as decision-making processes were concerned, the support staff contributed to on-going debates about encouraging greater use of learning technologies to help SEN pupils in the near future.

(ii) Crescent Secondary School

Distributed leadership was interpreted within the formal, organizational structure of the school. There were Directors of Learning who oversaw a faculty and Curriculum

Leaders, who might take charge of a department or a Key Stage. The lines of responsibility were clear and so were the processes of monitoring and evaluation. Surveys among teachers, support staff and pupils all indicated that they felt part of the decision-making processes. One of the arrangements that facilitated this was that on one day each week the timetable was curtailed one hour early so that staff could engage in CPD. The pupils might participate in extra-curricular activities such as sport, which were run by outside agencies. It was recognized that the training for support teachers had to be of a high quality if their work was going to produce the best results.

(iii) Grange Secondary School

Charles, the deputy headteacher, noted that staff at all levels and pupils had the opportunity to lead their own learning so, to that extent, leadership was highly distributed. Pupils were given evaluations to complete and the time needed to reflect on their own learning. Staff were consulted to find out about in which areas of teaching and learning they felt they needed further support. Charles chaired the 'Teaching and Learning' group, where teachers were able to discuss what was currently important to them. There was also a 'Teaching and Learning' impact group, which staff with no designated responsibilities or who were second in the department attended. He considered that such staff had a heavy teaching commitment and up-to-date knowledge of what was going on in the classroom.

Form tutors and pupils planned Citizenship days, which occurred six times a year, together, and pupils were closely involved in the planning. For a recent Citizenship day, the pupils had been given a brief about setting up a cafe. Charles described this process in the following way:

> They can decide as a form group the roles they are going to perform. Who is going to research? Who will be part of the management team? Who will do the advertising? Then they are given advice from their form tutors to see how they can best fulfil the roles they need to do. We say: 'This is what the end product, what we'd like it to be.' How can you best get there?

He argued that pupil voice was well developed within the school. For example, the school council decided what charity work the pupils would like to be involved in. Pupil voice was also evident through the use of Moodle (the school's virtual learning environment), where ideas could be shared. The pupils could also email staff about any issues with their work. Perhaps this was a way for some pupils to admit to not understanding something about their work if they did not have the confidence to speak to the member of staff.

The involvement of TAs in decision-making was very prominent at the classroom level, when there would be ongoing dialogue with the class teacher about how the TA might best help pupils with their learning difficulties.

(iv) Beehive Secondary School

Paul, the assistant headteacher, argued that the school was trying to move away from a 'top-down' approach to leadership and he described 'pockets' of distributed leadership within the school. He argued that the headteacher recognized that other staff could have good ideas, even though he was the one who could ultimately affect the progress of any proposed change. The current school improvement focus was on assessment for learning (AfL) (Black and Wiliam, 1998). The working party dealing with this contained members from across the school spectrum and they were able to make recommendations to the SLT and governors. Anyone who expressed an interest could be part of the working party and all members had an equal voice. An issue such as AfL was cross-curricular, and that tended to reduce the tensions involved (possibly between individual staff or between subject departments) because the policy was being developed for the whole school.

The degree to which leadership could be distributed reflected the culture of the school in terms of whether it had an open culture or not; i.e. 'Were the opinions of staff valued?' 'Were staff being empowered to take responsibility?' To some extent, that depended on whether the SLT were prepared to devolve such responsibilities or not. Paul remarked that: 'it is a leap of faith to let go of things'.

Paul explained the process of whole school policy formation and decision-making in relation to AfL:

> We had 40 colleagues actually involved in formulating the policy, taking the decisions that were then enacted. Obviously there was a check made by the senior management team that it wasn't outlandish what they were suggesting, but ultimately nothing changed. It was exactly as the staff wanted it to be.

Similarly, pupils were consulted on things like which charities they wanted to collect money for and what reward system should be set up across the school. In addition, other strategies were used to get feedback from pupils, including interviews with targeted groups of pupils, questionnaires with whole year groups and 'Survey Monkey', which contained online feedback from pupils.

TAs tended to have their views represented by either heads of department or the SENCO. The school had recently held an in-service training event based on improving pupils' emotional intelligence, which had been of particular benefit to TAs.

School Improvement: Recent Involvement in Educational Initiatives

(i) Quarry Secondary School

Michael, the deputy headteacher, noted a recent change in the leadership approach from one of measuring and analyzing performance to one of a more coaching-based strategy with the appointment of three Learning and Teaching Consultants (all internal appointments) as the school moved forward in fulfilling its aim of becoming an 'outstanding' school. Coaching was seen to be less about knowledge providing and more about facilitating discussions with teachers so they could take more ownership for themselves either individually as a group. These could be termed 'learning conversations' with the aim of teachers becoming more creative in their pedagogy. Michael described this ambitious process as follows:

> Learning conversations are filtering out not just from the senior leadership team but in all teams across the school. Learning conversations are two way: this is what we would like to do. As a team, what is it we ought to be doing? What is it that has been trialled? We are trying to facilitate that creativity at grass roots level. Many of our staff are now saying: Look, I want to trial this. They then bring it back to the table and say: 'I tried this pilot – it has been successful. I would like to do this is a team effort.'

Quarry school was also revising its policy on inclusion. The changes envisaged were intended to be introduced in September 2010 and involved revising the use of TAs in order to develop a new teaching and learning centre. Its function was threefold: (i) some TAs were to be designated to work with able and talented pupils; (ii) some TAs were to work with SEN pupils; (c) some TAs were to help move pupils who were not progressing with their learning and remained 'stuck' forward. A number of TAs would be allocated to subject teams and their purpose was to 'close or narrow the gap' (DfES, 2007) for pupils who were not progressing as might be expected. Other TAs would be working one-to-one with individual pupils, dealing with child-specific needs. At the same time, it was about empowering middle leaders to take ownership of the full spectrum of learners in their subject areas. This approach was designed to ensure that all team leaders could make appropriate provision for the full spectrum of learners in their curriculum area.

Quarry school had a small team of nominated 'pupil investigators' who could be called together to give feedback to staff on a range of initiatives in the school at any given time. They could be treated as a focus group, to give a student voice within the school improvement process. These investigators were proposed by staff or they were invited to apply. They were not elected, as would be the case for representatives for the School Council.

There were two specific projects to enrich the curriculum, raise aspirations and contribute to school improvement. One involved 50 Year 7 pupils who participated in a residential trip to a local university. These pupils were selected from families that would not necessarily have had any aspirations to encourage their son/daughter to apply for higher education. These pupils were able to mix with university students who had come from similar backgrounds to themselves.

A second project involved about 20 GCSE pupils working on a design project with a local car manufacturing company. The main task was to design an accessory for their most recently produced car. The pupils also visited the site to see how the design team worked.

Heather and Caroline were teachers of English and had both been appointed as teaching and learning consultants in Quarry school in the last three years. Heather noted that there had been a specific focus on the use of APP (Assessing Pupils' Progress) in the teaching of English recently. The use of this tool had helped make learning more personalized for the individual learner, particularly in terms of the skill development required in reading, listening, speaking and writing. It had helped with planning lessons and monitoring pupils' progress. It had benefits in other Core subjects and in the foundation subjects (e.g. history) as well.

Heather had also been involved in another initiative called 'Making Good Progress' (an initiative funded by the previous government) where pupils in Key Stage 3 (usually Years 7 or 8) received ten hours extra tuition in English or maths. The pupils targeted were perceived to be 'stuck' at level 5 and individual staff had signed up to do this work.

Caroline noted that AfL was the most influential initiative as it had the biggest impact in terms helping pupils to know where they were with their learning, where they were going and, most importantly of all, how they were going to get there. AfL had helped produce a cultural shift towards students being able to take more responsibility for their own learning.

(ii) Crescent Secondary School

The major focus in Crescent school recently had been to move from being classed as a 'good' school to being judged as 'outstanding' by Ofsted. Claire, the assistant headteacher, discussed this achievement in the following way:

> Last year was about setting pupils more challenging tasks. In becoming outstanding, obviously one of the key things is about risk-taking, pupils being inspired; then having choice in their learning so in terms of lessons, we have encouraged that a little bit more. This is the outcome; it does not matter how you get there – this way, that way, actually doing some training on that. Getting staff to value the process and letting students had some choice in that.

This process involved pupils making more decisions for themselves about their learning and becoming more independent. It also meant encouraging staff to be willing to take some risks and move out of their 'comfort zones'.

The SLT in Crescent school discovered from pupil surveys that some staff were spending too much lesson time talking. One technique that was tried out was to challenge teachers not to use more than 20 spoken words in a lesson. That meant teachers had to find other ways of giving feedback and limit their oral exposition.

Suzie (acting head of English) was involved in developing agreed protocols in different subject areas for group activities. If this could be agreed across the school, in all the subject areas, it would mean that group roles were assigned the same names (e.g. chairperson, secretary etc.) so that pupils could work together more easily to develop their transferable skills (e.g. problem solving; creativity; collaboration). The pupils also needed to be very clear about what was expected of them as individuals in any group activity.

Robert, head of geography, had done some research on the views of pupils, parents and staff about the potential benefits of using a virtual learning environment (e.g. Moodle) both in school and outside school time. He found that it was only really beneficial for pupils if it was used for extended learning outside school hours. In school, pupils engaged more with their learning without the use of Moodle. This appeared to be because they wanted to interact more with the teacher in school. This possibly made differentiation easier to achieve as the teacher knew what to say to help the pupil. Outside school, the pupils were given projects, which they could do over the summer holidays.

Another initiative involved the tracking of pupil progress where, within a given level (e.g. level 5), it was broken down into sub-sections and the pupils' end-of-year targets were colour-coded so both the pupils and their parents could understand more clearly whether the pupil was on track, progressing as expected, or falling behind.

(iii) Grange Secondary School

Charles, the deputy headteacher, felt that all staff were actively encouraged to be involved with initiatives. If a member of staff proposed an idea, then it would be discussed in an SLT meeting. That teacher would then receive some feedback, making sure that that person felt that his or her ideas were being listened to.

One innovative strategy was for teachers to support their colleagues in other departments and share ideas: i.e. history with design and technology; MFL (modern foreign languages) with music. A given member of staff may not have any specialism in the other subject but was recognized by the SLT as being an effective teacher and possibly could be the catalyst for improving standards of teaching and learning in the other subject area. The focus was possibly on situations where pupils were responding well in one subject area but generating problems in another.

Sonia (acting executive head of music and a languages specialist) had recently been involved in supporting efforts to improve teaching and learning in a local grammar school and another local secondary school. Grange school had been recommended by the LEA to other local schools when they had not done well in their own Ofsted inspection. Staff from these schools had visited Grange school and observed classroom practice. Occasional problems had been generated, though, when teachers from Grange school made reciprocal visits to other schools and had not been made welcome initially. It was noted that one of the deputy headteachers in another school who had visited Grange school on a number of occasions did really seem appreciate the opportunity to observe and discuss the pedagogical approaches used.

Pam, the head of history and executive head of design and technology, discussed a recent initiative in relation to her 'support' work in the design and technology department, which could be described as a 'fragmented' department whose GCSE examination results were not as good as they might be. The headteacher had set aside four periods a week for this work. Although Pam was a history specialist, her forte in her own subject was seen as having a very positive influence on results and having ideas about how to get pupils interested in the subject.

Pam thought that one of her first objectives would be to ensure that each member of the design and technology staff felt valued. She had carried out some individual interviews with staff and also had offered support in lessons. The focus was on Year 11 pupils, to try and boost their GCSE results.

(iv) Beehive Secondary School

It had been decided that every member of staff would be placed in a learning team from September 2010, to continue the school improvement focus on AfL (as mentioned earlier). The team would be cross-curricular, involving five or six members of staff. They would be expected to meet regularly and do some peer observation, and joint lesson planning would also be encouraged.

Jill (an advanced skills teacher and head of Spanish) was currently working on promoting learning within the school. One problem with the existing 'Teaching and Learning' group was that faculties would send representatives to the meetings, but whatever was discussed and agreed was not necessarily relayed to other staff, so she felt that improving learning (especially literacy) needed to be part of every member of staff's job description. As a pilot, she had gathered together about 20 key members of staff to meet together twice every half term. The group contained a mix of ages, gender and experience. The focus for each half term had included discussion, writing lesson objectives and giving feedback to pupils. In the academic year 2010–2011, everyone would be allocated to a learning team of about five or six staff, led by one of the pilot team members, who would be the co-ordinator. The focus would be on improving literacy across the school, which might include developing better reading skills and improving writing skills.

Leading The Learning: Teachers' Work with Pupils

(i) Quarry Secondary School

Michael, the deputy headteacher, was of the opinion that there was more of a move towards giving opportunities for pupils to lead their own learning in lessons, to some extent. This was changing the teacher's role to become more of a facilitator of learning, shaping ideas and helping pupils interrogate a range of solutions to problems. This was also being promoted as a way of developing leadership skills among pupils.

Caroline and Heather were both teachers of English as well as being 'Teaching and Learning Consultants' in the school. To build a culture of shared values and collaboration, Caroline tried to model good behaviour; set clear expectations, which would be made explicit to the pupils; treat pupils equitably; and actively demonstrate that she attached value to every pupil's contribution. Similarly, Heather highlighted the importance of modelling not only in terms of behaviour but also showing pupils how they might approach a specific task. For example, at the start of Year 10 in GCSE English, she would model how to do a presentation in front of the class by doing one about herself first. She would then ask each pupil to do a presentation, when she could assess each individual's skills in speaking and listening.

To try and help pupils learn effectively, Heather used active learning techniques such as reading a passage all together out loud to try and minimize pupils' problems with pronunciation. She would ask each pupil to read one word at a time or whisper one line, then shout the next line.

When introducing Shakespearian text to Year 10 GCSE classes, which can be very confusing for pupils, Heather often used the following strategy:

> I might not even mention that it is Shakespeare to start with: I might just use some text on the interactive whiteboard ... I tell them it is 'text-speak' or something like that and then get them to try and work out what it means. I tell them they do not have to understand every word; just get a feel for it and tell me. Then I tell them they have been studying Shakespeare and how brilliant they all are because they understood what he was trying to say.

Caroline was very keen on the use of differentiation strategies and personalized target setting, as well as providing a suitably challenging task for pupils to help their learning to progress. She referred to a SEN pupil who was autistic, which made it difficult to assess that pupil's speaking and listening skills. A podcast was used from which the pupil was able to create an individual presentation, which Caroline could give feedback on.

(ii) Crescent Secondary School

As was referred to earlier, there was encouragement from the SLT in the school for teachers to set more challenging tasks and take more risks with their lesson planning. This was also about giving the pupils more choice in the way they went about a task in order to obtain a balance between too much 'scaffolding' (i.e. spoon feeding) and too little, which might result in the pupils not being able to cope.

Robert, head of geography, commented on the importance of letting the pupils know that the teacher was learning alongside them. It was also important to speak to every pupil during a lesson. That simple element increased pupils' respect for the teacher. It was easier often to highlight what had been learned in terms of knowledge as compared to skills. Making decisions on the basis of weighing up the potential benefits of various options occurred quite frequently in a subject like geography.

Michael had recently been involved in teaching a topic where the pupils themselves had designed the scheme of work. This had taken place just after the earthquake had struck in Haiti, so the pupils decided which aspects of geography they would like to focus upon in that context. This approach reflected a desire among some staff to try and develop more independence in terms of the learning of the pupils. The emphasis in geography was to try and develop pupils as more creative thinkers, reflective enquirers and independent learners.

According to Suzie (acting AST and an English teacher), all the pupils were accustomed to the use of the Accelerated Learning Cycle (ALC), one part of which was spending ten minutes at the end of a lesson reflecting on what they had learned, reviewing what they had done and how they had done it. ALC had been adopted as a whole school policy and had four phases. Suzie referred to this as:

> the four-part lesson cycle links the lesson to previous learning; activates the learning; pupils demonstrating their learning and the teacher then consolidating it.

Suzie felt that building a culture of shared values with pupils was sometimes problematic. She cited an example of her Year 11 group that contained a large proportion of Afro-Caribbean students, basing her comments on their behaviour at home.

> One of the things I found particularly interesting recently was about Caribbean students. The way they communicate at home in families is largely everyone speaking at the same time. In most classrooms, talking at the same time as everyone else is not how you want it to work. But they can listen to multiple voices and talk at the same time … My values are that they

should be quiet and listen to someone speaking – as soon as I stopped doing that and did not treat it as deliberately disrespectful and disruptive behaviour it became much more relaxed. The behaviour improved.

It therefore had become more difficult for these pupils to adapt to a classroom culture where listening was considered to be desirable when someone else was expressing an opinion.

Suzie had been involved in a 'Connecting Classrooms' joint project that consisted of three schools in the local area in the UK, three schools in Ghana and three schools in South Africa. The projects were funded by the British Council and one aspect that may have an impact in the future in school was pupils taking on leadership roles, such as being a literacy leader. It was intended that pupils in Year 9 would become literacy leaders and visit local primary schools to teach some literacy lessons, for which they would get an award (a certificate).

(iii) Grange Secondary School

From an SLT perspective, Charles discussed classroom approaches that emphasized metacognitive processes; i.e. pupils reflecting more on their own thinking processes. Pupils also focused on memorizing information and ways of helping them remember things more easily; placing events in sequence and remembering what actions they had taken from a chronological perspective. Personalized targets were important: i.e. rather than voicing an opinion, encouraging pupils to back it up with some evidence. Such targets were discussed with form tutors regularly during the year.

As far as building a culture of shared values and collaboration with pupils was concerned, Sonia considered that is was a judicious mix of paying close attention to classroom details combined with a whole school ethos that was important. As can be seen in the following quote, her ideas are based on some previous experience teaching in another school:

It does have to do with the whole school ethos. I've worked in a school where there hasn't been a high level of expectation and what you do in your classroom is very difficult when it's not represented by the teachers as a whole school ethos. In terms of a teacher in a classroom, it's about consistency; it's about linking everything you do in with the wider school if there is a strong ethos; it's about expectations; it's about well-planned lessons; it's about listening to pupils; communicating with pupils; appreciating their background, their culture and what they want to do in the future. It's about the bigger picture and how you fit into it and how you can make your subject relevant to them.

For Sonia, maintaining clear boundaries was also a key aspect as well as being approachable, open and honest. Developing the pupils' key skills, such as analysis, evaluation and thinking skills, could be incorporated easily into any task, but the intended development of these skills needed to be made clear to the pupils.

Pam (head of history and executive head of design and technology) placed some emphasis on re-stating level descriptors in pupil-friendly language in history. She stated that:

> They've done a recent assessment on the Civil War using two newspapers where one is written from one perspective and the other is written from a different perspective. If the pupils write from one perspective only they can only get a certain level but if they can understand both perspectives, then they would achieve a higher level.

Pupils could set their own personal targets based on agreed success criteria, so they were aware of what might make a good piece of work. Peer assessment was used extensively to see what might be good about another pupil's work and how that might influence the assessor's own work in the future.

With SEN pupils, Pam felt that setting achievable targets with an individual pupil was very important. She placed particular emphasis on building confidence with the use of sentence starters and verbal recording work on tape recorders. There was a great deal of encouragement for these SEN pupils to write one line and speak it out loud. She also used PowerPoint, where pupils were encouraged to add in their own words on a single slide.

(iv) Beehive Secondary School

Paul, the assistant headteacher, argued that a culture of shared values and collaboration existed in Beehive school and was one of its strengths. Values such as honesty, respect, democracy and integrity were not seen as mutually exclusive but all played a key part in the holistic development of the child. Ideally, it would be very desirable for pupils to develop more independence in their learning, and that was being encouraged through the continuing use of AfL. However, there were pressures due to accountability, which could lead to a degree of tension for classroom teachers, between encouraging pupils to be more independent and meeting the requirements of accountability, usually driven by central government.

A system had been used successfully to boost the attainment of Year 11 pupils. It was a database-driven process where every half term the pupils were assessed by the staff on a T, T+ or T- system, which indicated whether they were on target to achieve their expected GCSE grade, doing better than that or doing less well than expected. This was called the Progression Achievement Leader (PAL) process and involved every pupil meeting up with a senior member of staff to discuss his or her progress. Paul met up with between 25 and 20 pupils each half term. They were removed from lessons for about ten minutes to have this discussion.

The feedback from the pupils appeared to be very positive as they felt the teachers were taking more interest in them. The scheme was also going to be extended so that pupils could grade themselves, so self-reporting could become an important part of the process of pupils leading their own learning. It appeared that the biggest impact to date had been with some of the male pupils. These pupils, usually with a number of T- grades had been receiving extra help after school from the appropriate staff.

Jill (AST and head of Spanish) described her involvement with using targets within the PAL system. She noted that:

> if you engage with those targets, it does make you (as the teacher) very reflective … and we devise support materials to help them reach those targets.

One advantage was that if an able child handed in a rushed piece of work or had not pushed him or herself to the standard that might be expected, that pupil could be graded as T-.

A technique that could be used to help pupils learn effectively would be to show them a piece of work of a high standard as a model and then this could be broken down to pinpoint which elements were good. The pupils themselves could then use some aspects, incorporated into their own work. Jill also stressed the use of targets to enable students to be aware of success criteria, which influenced the quality of their own work.

Teacher Collaboration with Other Teachers and Support Staff

(i) Quarry Secondary School

Heather and Caroline were both teachers of English and Teaching and Learning Consultants in Quarry school. Heather noted the difficulties of working with some other more experienced staff, especially when trying to encourage others to use the APP system (DCSF, 2010) for personalized learning (referred to in Chapter 4). Part of her ability to build a culture of collaboration was to admit freely her own initial struggles with APP. She would then follow that up by explaining the ways she overcame these obstacles. She explained her work as a Teaching And Learning Consultant in the following way:

> All the Teaching and Learning Consultants have an open-door policy where if anybody wants to come and observe they can just come in. Other than that, staff can come to us and say 'I really need some help with peer assessment,' then we'll arrange for them to come and observe one of us, or to observe another member of staff at school that we know is good at peer assessment … You will never win every battle, but I think that perseverance to try and

show the good and bad sides of everything; give them solutions to any problems that they might come across; being a good listener, being able to negotiate with them, encouraging them … I would never ask somebody to do something that I haven't tried myself. It's being seen to be doing the right thing. If people can see you're doing it yourself, then they are a little bit more encouraged to give it a go.

Everything was based on having established trust, credibility and good working relationships, as well as being willing to persevere in the face of difficulties. Heather considered that it was necessary to be good at negotiating, listening and encouraging other staff.

Caroline observed many staff teaching different subjects, and they could observe her teach at any time as well. She offered 'drop-in' opportunities normally after school one day a week so that individual staff, from any subject discipline, could plan to improve an aspect of practice: for example, the use of group work or formative assessment.

(ii) Crescent Secondary School

Robert, as head of geography, found himself in the position of having two new staff appointed to his department after only one year in full-time teaching himself. This meant they could determine subject priorities through a process of sharing ideas and consultation. However, this was a complex situation, as there were two other staff who taught geography part time and who were both assistant headteachers with whole school responsibilities. Their attendance at departmental meetings was sporadic, although they were supportive and did come to meetings that were concerned with reviewing the curriculum or the construction of a departmental action plan.

Sharing ideas with other humanities teachers was more complex. For example, the history teachers in the school were long established, having taught in the school for between 15 and 30 years, and their teaching methods were very different from the ones used in geography.

Claire noted that time was probably the main barrier to teacher collaboration, but the fact that staff could meet together for one and half hours one afternoon each week minimized that barrier to some extent.

(iii) Grange Secondary School

Sonia (languages teacher and executive head of music) noted the difficulties of working in a collegial fashion in a subject department like music where she had no real specialism. There were two music specialists in the school but they both had other, more senior roles. The permanent head of music was on maternity leave but had previously struggled to delegate and obtain full co-operation from her colleagues at times. Sonia had been able to generate a more pleasant working atmosphere and was also able to draw on practice from other departments she had worked in. She did admit to finding it hard to pin the assessment procedures down in Music. This had resulted in pupils having a rather negative attitude towards the subject itself, as they were often unaware of the next steps in their learning. The two music specialist staff felt it was not their job to sort out schemes of work and develop consistent and robust assessment procedures.

There were additional difficulties when trying to develop greater collaboration with support assistants as they did not get any PPA time and were occupied throughout the day in classes. Much of the planning with TAs occurred on an ad hoc basis, often in a ten-minute 'window' during a lesson.

Pam, as head of history, commented that there was a great deal of sharing of lesson plans. History staff might take responsibility for mini-schemes of work, which were then shared amongst everyone else. Individual staff sometimes did presentations in departmental meetings. The ICT facilities were very good, with all the history staff having access to rooms containing IWBs. Film clips could easily be shown to all classes as appropriate. Reliance on expensive textbooks was also greatly reduced.

Other examples of collaborative effort were related to historical events in America, which ultimately led to the fledgling civil rights movement gaining a great deal of publicity at the time. One particularly shocking incident was alluded to by Pam where a teenage boy called Emmett Till was killed for making a joke about going out with a white girl. One member of Pam's department had contacted the Emmett Till Society for further information.

Charles, deputy headteacher, considered that any potential barriers were obstacles to be overcome. He noted that:

> It's all down to personal drive. If you want to collaborate with someone then you collaborate with them. If there are any barriers, then it is my job to remove them or help someone with it. No obstacle is insurmountable.

(iv) Beehive Secondary School

Jill (AST and head of Spanish) felt that it was very important to avoid e-mailing staff where at all possible. She considered that a face-to-face, personal interaction was far more likely to generate positive support for an initiative. Referring to pilot work done in the school earlier, Jill noted that she divided up the responsibilities for each aspect of AfL among the group members so that one teacher was responsible for developing different forms of questioning techniques to be used by staff; one for what makes good learning outcomes; one teacher looked at aspects of differentiation etc. She felt all the staff enjoyed doing some academic research, which could then be shared with the rest of the group.

Jill was involved in developing language skills in primary schools. One example of teacher collaboration was a teacher in Jill's department who initiated a Tour de France activity, which meant that 70 children from local primary schools could come into Beehive school for a day and do a languages activity in the morning and then go out on the school field where a very large map of France was laid out. All the major cities were clearly marked on this map. The pupils, in small groups, were then able to move around from one city to another, where they would undertake a challenge or task in each city. Two examples of pupils' tasks might be: (i) work out how many Euros you need to exchange for an overnight stay in the city; or (ii) learn a finger rhyme in Paris and then perform it in the French language.

Teacher support for any whole school policy usually depends on how it is interpreted. As a consequence, it is sometimes not always implemented in the ways that have been agreed. Paul, as a member of the SLT, was asked by the headteacher to find out whether all staff were actually doing what they had been asked to do in relation to AfL. The school had previously a lot of time on running INSET days on AfL and focusing on student feedback. What was found was that some staff were clearly not following what had been agreed, so a system of 'learning walks' was instituted. This involved the head of faculty/head of department/head of Key Stage walking around the school with a member of the SLT to observe practice in lessons for themselves. Observation in the lessons included examining three or four exercise books and noting the comments made by staff.

Teacher collaboration could be limited if learning teams were attended by subject representatives who felt obligated to attend and did not 'buy' into the emphasis on improving learning. Paul noted:

> We are aware that with a large staff, not everyone will buy into it, but if you get 70 to 80 per cent of the staff involved, that will bring real improvement.

Working in Partnership with Parents

(i) Quarry Secondary School

Regular phone calls home were made to discuss a pupil's learning, especially if he or she appeared to be making little or no progress. Often Heather (Teaching and Learning Consultant and teacher of English) would send home revision guides at the request of the parents. On occasions, when a pupil's parents did not speak much English, there would be contact through older siblings or, if necessary, access to a translator funded by the local authority. In the Core subjects, the efforts and achievement of a pupil could be recognized, and a letter sent home to celebrate being a 'Star in English/maths'.

A workshop was run for the parents of gifted and talented pupils, which focused on trying to provide them with ideas about activities that could be done at home with their son/daughter.

(ii) Crescent Secondary School

Claire, assistant headteacher, described the way in which a learning night for parents was conducted. This was targeted at those Year 11 pupils on the GCSE grade C/D borderline and was a workshop for parents 'to help them guide their children to learn'. About one third of the parents attended this event. It was felt to be important that parents knew what to expect from the revision process: for example, not having a revision book, the subject was hard for some parents to understand, but conversely they should understand the rationale and processes involved when their son/daughter was doing practice examination questions.

(iii) Grange Secondary School

Charles, the deputy headteacher, noted the importance of parent partnerships, which were linked to pupil progress. The school had a community centre and literacy classes ran during the day for parents. Other activities such as Arabic speaking classes would take place during and after school. Turnout for parents' evenings was very good and in some cases could reach 90 per cent. Charles felt that this was due to the positive relationships that had been built up over a long period of time. Communication with parents involved letters home. Phone calls and texts were also used as reminders.

(iv) Beehive Secondary School

Jill (AST and head of Spanish) felt that all parents intended to help their children in one way or another but not everyone was able to make time. She asked parents to test their children on specific vocabulary. She sometimes asked the pupils to sign their homework, or she might say:

Teach your parent/brother/sister this and get your parent to sign that you have done it.

What Does This Evidence Indicate About Teachers Taking Responsibility for Teaching and Learning?

(i) Support for teacher leadership

Whilst support from SLTs in the schools visited for teacher leadership was apparent, this was perceived to be within a culture of quality assurance and accountability. This meant that teacher leadership had to operate within the school's hierarchical structure (Busher, 2006) and take account of formal line management responsibilities. Nevertheless,

SLTs would empower staff to take worthwhile risks (Harris, 2004). In Grange school, staff with no line management responsibilities could participate in the Teaching and Learning Impact Group. Involvement in decision-making was evident in the all the schools visited, especially in relation to consultation (Day and Harris, 2003). However, it was not entirely clear as to whether the opinions of all stakeholders (i.e. pupils, parents and staff) were all of equal value.

(ii) School improvement

All schools made use of some government-funded initiatives to track pupils' progress (e.g. APP [DCSF, 2010]). One school (Crescent) had appointed three Teaching and Learning Consultants to engage in learning conversations with staff and they were also used in mentoring/coaching capacities (Pask and Joy, 2007). The same school was making efforts to develop more holistic transferable skills (i.e. PLTS [QCDA, 2009)] in its pupils.

All the teacher-leaders placed a great deal of emphasis on assessment for learning approaches and were encouraging pupils to take more responsibility for their own learning (Harris, 2007).

Grange school was using an innovative school improvement strategy by encouraging teachers from one subject department who were deemed to be successful, effective and established members of staff to act in a support role in subject teaching in another department whose examination results reflected a degree of underperformance in the subject.

Quarry school had recently changed the ways in which its TAs were deployed so that they could help to raise the standards of teaching and learning across the whole ability range.

(iii) Teacher-leaders working with pupils

Regarding building a culture of shared values and collaboration with pupils, teacher-leaders were fully aware of the need to model desirable behaviour in front of pupils in the classroom. Attaching value to the contributions made by all pupils was important. Modelling good practice in terms of how to approach specific tasks (e.g. giving a presentation in public) was regarded as very effective. All the teacher-leaders interviewed were unanimous about letting pupils know that they were learners as well (Durrant and Holden, 2006).

Several teacher-leaders in the schools visited referred to the need to set challenging tasks appropriate to each pupil and to take justifiable risks with new pedagogical approaches to learning, even if it meant moving out of the 'comfort zone'.

An interesting issue was raised by Suzie in Crescent school and highlighted the cultural differences between what might be acceptable in relation to pupils' communication skills such as speaking and listening at home and what might be acceptable in school, especially in group activities and whole-class discussion.

Sonia (in Grange school) noted the difficulties that arise for the classroom teacher when there is an absence of a positive whole school ethos and a lack of emphasis on learning. She had experienced this in a previous school.

In terms of sharing values and collaborating with pupils, it was suggested that clear expectations, equity, modelling the desired behaviour and valuing the contributions made by the pupils were all important (Watkins et al., 2007). Modelling was also very useful when it came to pupils themselves deciding why a specific piece of work might be considered to be of a high standard. (Southworth, 2004).

Other aspects of working with pupils included an emphasis on the teacher as a facilitator of learning, which meant that, as in the case of Crescent school, the pupils had the opportunity to design their own scheme of work. This is what O'Donoghue and Clarke (2010) refer to as self-regulated learning.

The metacognitive aspects of learning (Dimmock, 2000) were deemed to be important, giving pupils the opportunity to reflect upon their own learning. Developing pupils' metacognitive abilities was stressed strongly in several schools visited (Durrant and Holden, 2006).

Beehive school had developed an effective tracking and tutorial system, giving Year 11 pupils every chance to achieve their target GCSE grades. It also enabled able and talented pupils to be pushed harder if their work-level performance dipped below that which they could achieve.

A great deal of support was given by the teacher-leaders to the effectiveness of using AfL techniques.

(iv) Teacher-leaders working collaboratively with other staff

In Crescent school, staff could meet one afternoon a week to plan collaborative projects (Busher, 2006; Frost and Durrant, 2003).

Responsibility for joint curriculum planning (Gunter, 2005) was noted in Beehive Secondary School, where collaboration on an AfL project had been very successful through a 'division of labour' approach.

The Teaching and Learning Consultants interviewed in Quarry school both emphasized the importance of negotiating with staff as well as listening and encouraging them (Harris and Muijs, 2005). They also helped out in a mentoring role with less-experienced colleagues. These consultants were not over-burdened by other demanding whole school responsibilities.

A number of 'barriers' to teacher collaboration were noted: i.e. lack of time; the limitations that are imposed if some staff do not 'buy into' school improvement efforts, with the result that the agreed policy was not implemented in the classroom; meeting up with TAs when they were fully occupied during the working day; and working with two senior staff in a subject department like maths, which was difficult to organize.

(v) Teachers working with parents

Communication with parents was a very important element in all the schools visited, but schools used different approaches depending on their specific local circumstances. For example, Quarry school, which had a higher proportion of EAL pupils, used a sibling or a translator to help develop and maintain lines of communication with the school. Another school (Grange) was used as a community centre during the day, which helped to develop relationships with parents. The schools also placed a great deal of emphasis on celebrating pupils' achievements.

Leading the Learning in Secondary Schools in Wales

10

Distributed Leadership: SLT Perspectives

(i) Valley Secondary School

Although there was strong support for the idea of distributed leadership from the SLT, the school was running a deficit budget in 2009–2010, and this had resulted in there being less input from staff in decision-making processes. The support manager (who was the line manager for the office staff, technicians etc.) and the school's SENCO (who line managed the TAs) were both members of the school's SLT, giving them an important 'voice'. Having stated that, the role of middle leaders such as heads of subject departments was now more developed, as they had been given more responsibility to influence classroom practice indirectly. In a previous inspection in 2006, Estyn had noted that the role of head of department was underdeveloped. Since then, a Curriculum Board (attended by those with teaching and learning responsibilities) had been set up to discuss issues directly related to teaching and learning: for example, Curriculum Cymreig, homework, working with able and talented pupils etc. Each issue would subsequently be discussed in more depth in departmental meetings as the main item under discussion.

(ii) Waters Edge Secondary School

According to Gareth, the deputy headteacher, the notion of teachers leading the learning both with pupils in the classroom and in support of other colleagues had slowly developed over the last five years. There had been a gradual shift towards giving pupils more opportunities to lead their own learning with the teacher as a facilitator. This was despite a legacy of prescription within the National Curriculum that had characterized education policy in the last 25 years; i.e. a top-down approach that had led to a certain cultural attitude among some teachers. This could be summed up as: 'Tell me what to do and how I am going to do it.' Fortunately, the proportion of staff with this attitude was diminishing. Gareth felt that placing pupil learning at the heart of what the school was doing was the result of 'creating the culture, creating the momentum and then changing the practice'.

Decision-making in the classroom was a key element in improving teaching and learning by allowing pupils to be as involved as possible with making decisions about their own learning. Gareth made an important distinction between 'learner voice' and 'pupil voice', placing much more emphasis on the importance of learner voice. Pupil voice was useful in some contexts, for example, school councils; pupils being involved in selection panels for new staff; using pupil survey information when considering changes to lunchtime arrangements etc. However, learner voice was far more about the individual pupil making choices about his or her own learning in the classroom.

(iii) Hillside Secondary School

According to Sian, the deputy headteacher, leadership was distributed throughout the school quite extensively. Within the SLT there were clearly defined roles and responsibilities. Heads of department and heads of year had a great deal of autonomy when doing their jobs. All staff were encouraged to lead various initiatives, which often meant leading teams of their colleagues. The school had employed a 'transition co-ordinator' over the last three years who was expected to lead teams of colleagues in the school as well as feeder primary schools.

Staff were always invited to express their interest in being involved in initiatives and sometimes Sian would approach a particular person who would be suitable and may wish to be involved, with this being flagged up as a useful staff development opportunity.

Pupils were involved in decision-making processes at a whole school level, especially when it came to interviewing new staff. Hillside school used sixth formers to help with this process as it was felt that they were more likely to make a mature decision.

Consultation with staff tended to be done in small groups with their line managers, as meetings involving the whole staff did not always prove to be very effective.

Support staff received a great deal of training when they first started in the school. They went through a performance management process and were observed in the classroom working with the pupils so that any weaknesses could be identified. Each member of the support staff tended to be assigned to a specific pupil with learning difficulties.

(iv) Eastside Secondary School

Rhodri, the deputy headteacher, considered distribution of leadership to be role-orientated and delegation of leadership to be task-orientated. He noted that the role of the classroom teacher was central to leading the learning, and pupils could play their part as well. He felt that good decision-making was predicated on values such as respect, trust and good communication. Underpinning this was a supportive culture/ethos within the school.

The enhancement of pupil voice was to be a central feature in Eastside in 2010–2011, with the adoption of a project called 'Learning Detectives'. This was piloted in 2009–2010 and involved pupils going into lessons as observers. Rhodri sounded a note of caution about this process:

> You can see that this could be a threat to some teachers so it has to be done very sensitively. The aim of it is to give pupils a bigger voice in what they are seeing and how they perceive lessons, to get them much more involved in the whole process of their learning.

The pilot was carried out with volunteer staff. The pupils themselves needed to be trained carefully and the whole process was carefully structured. The pupils' comments were anonymized and they were told not to comment in any negative way about the lesson. Instead, they were only to comment on what they had enjoyed, in order to stimulate a dialogue with the teacher. One of the potential offshoots of the 'Learning Detectives' initiative might be that pupils would have more empathy for staff who deal with the learning needs of 30 pupils on a daily basis.

In addition, many subject departments already asked pupils to feed back to them at the end of a topic. What went well? What was less successful? What could be improved? How would they change things?

School Improvement: Recent Involvement in Educational Initiatives

(i) Valley Secondary School

There was encouragement for all staff to become involved in educational initiatives but this came through the line management system, which acted as a 'filter'. Natasha, the deputy headteacher, argued that any proposals for school improvement initiatives could initially be referred to the relevant line manager as a first course of action, since they could then be modified as a result of discussion. One of the most recent initiatives had been for some staff to have an involvement with the University of the First Age, where the challenge was to try and be more creative in their teaching. It was targeted at improving pupils' key skills.

According to Jason, head of maths, accelerated learning had been used with Year 7 pupils and with feeder primary school pupils. In addition, the Assessing Pupils' Progress (APP) programme was being introduced in the subject teaching in order to try and bring about greater consistency in a large department of nine staff, where three were specialist maths teachers who were full-time and six other staff who taught maths alongside other commitments.

(ii) Waters Edge Secondary School

Gareth, the deputy headteacher, explained the introduction of the 'Integrated Curriculum' in Year 7 two years ago. A team of ten part-volunteer and part-selected teachers with different subject backgrounds started to meet together regularly to plan the introduction of this new curriculum approach. This was timed to coincide with implementation of new National Curriculum subject orders in 2008 and a new Skills Framework (DECLLS, 2008b), which promoted skills ahead of knowledge and content.

Planning for the introduction of the Integrated Curriculum really began to move forward when it was realized that the key question was really 'What is it that the learners need in terms of the skills they need to develop?' Such an approach meant that teachers could take on a more professional role in developing the curriculum, alongside the associated responsibility and accountability. In order to placate those teachers who might have felt that children would not learn anything if they switched to a more skills-based pedagogy, the skills themselves were not subject-specific, but more broadly based and cross-curricular in nature – for example: finding things out and reporting; report writing and essay writing; questioning and analyzing.

Samantha was one of the form tutors involved and she explained that the Integrated Curriculum aimed to produce more autonomous, independent learners. The skills being developed included, for example, listening skills, extended writing, problem solving, asking questions and thinking skills. It placed a great deal of emphasis on pupils working in groups, reflecting on their learning through the use of 'think, pair, share' as well as using 'two stars and a wish' for commenting on their strengths and areas for development.

The Year 7 form tutors who taught the Integrated Curriculum worked with their pupils for four hours every two weeks and in Year 8 for three hours every two weeks. The classes worked to a theme that, for example, might be 'Life on the Edge'. This could mean on the edges of society or on the border between two countries – it could be interpreted in different curriculum areas in different ways. The scientific contribution to 'Life on the Edge' was for pupils to engage in a problem-solving exercise designing a container that would allow an egg to be dropped from a height of two metres without breaking. One pupil had decided to drop his egg into custard to see how well that worked!

A monitoring and evaluation system was set up to ensure that staff were constantly getting any feedback they might need. Such a system involved interviewing pupils, looking at exercise books and meeting regularly to pass around examples of pupils' work for comment. This was made easier because the lead focus was on skills-based learning, not improving subject knowledge and understanding. The Integrated Curriculum was continuing to develop, giving the learner a 'voice' about where the learning was going next. This meant that schemes of work could not be overly prescriptive.

Accountability in the form of assessment had been built in to the Year 7 curriculum. There were five topic areas, which each had an associated assessment that pupils tackled at the end of the topic. The teachers themselves could select in which way they wanted the pupils to demonstrate what they learned; for example, through the use of a dramatic performance, a data handling exercise, an extended piece of writing or a presentation. Gareth felt that a very important part of this process was moderation, so when all the work had been produced it was moderated by the team of teachers.

The recent introduction of the Welsh Baccalaureate in Key Stage 4 dovetailed well into existing practice in the school in relation to the development of key skills. For example, certificates for level two 'Communication' were already being issued for pupils who had successfully demonstrated the following elements: presentational skills, report writing skills, group work skills. Even before the Welsh Baccalaureate was introduced, the pupils already undertook their own investigations, thus its introduction was far smoother than it might have been. Gareth felt that one drawback associated with the Welsh Baccalaureate was the level of bureaucracy and form filling that needed to be done.

Gordon, an English teacher, was heavily involved with planning for the development of schemes of work for the Integrated Curriculum. He had offered specific support for some staff who lacked experience in using extended writing.

Gordon was involved in an after-school creative writing initiative called Muse, where all the participants (i.e. pupils in Year 7 right through to Year 13) shared what they had written within a forum for discussion and critique. A whole range of literary activities were covered, including prose, poetry and micro-fiction. Their work was then displayed for others to see.

(iii) Hillside Secondary School

As a result of some staff receiving training on the introduction of Building Learning Power (Claxton, 2002), the pupils were now being taught more about the learning process in PSE. This helped pupils by teaching them about *how* to learn and what to do when they were 'stuck'.

Chris, the head of PE, was concentrating his efforts on helping A level students fill out UCAS applications for entry into higher education. He commented that:

> We are asking the students to really analyze their choices, do their research, make sure they engage in some kind of peer and self-assessment before they ever get to the stage of making applications to universities.

He wanted the students to make choices that were more suited to their needs and for this *not* to be a process that was engaged in without much thought and planning. He wanted to encourage more personal self-reflection and self-evaluation. This had been reinforced in school with individual students meeting up with their tutors.

A recent initiative – an active young person's programme – funded by the local authority offered areas of curriculum enrichment that complemented what was currently being offered within PE. Among other things, it encouraged participation in a sport for the 'love' of that sport, on a recreational basis. The co-ordinator of the programme had introduced newer sports such as 'free running' a (combination of running, gymnastics and acrobatics), which had proved very popular among the pupils.

Zoe (head of English) had recently been involved with working within a local cluster of schools to introduce electronic storytelling as part of a transition project. This used a piece of software called 'Audacity and Movie-Maker', which allowed pupils to write a story in the first instance. They searched the Internet to find pictures to represent the story. They could then present their work electronically rather than as a more traditional piece of written work. It appeared that the boys had responded to this approach particularly well.

The English department had also been heavily involved with a 'Learning Journal' initiative, which encouraged pupils to reflect upon what they had learned and whether they had met their targets. These journals were updated every month and helped to keep the pupils focused on where their learning was going.

(iv) Eastside Secondary School

Eastside school used a system of TIPs (Team Improvement Plans) and SIPs (School Improvement Plans), which were intended to be aligned with each other. Departments had the freedom to take initiatives on, but there were some things that all subject areas had to deal with, as action points arising from the recent Estyn inspection. Rhodri, the deputy headteacher, felt that the school diary could become incredibly congested at certain times of the year and so suggested that some proposed initiatives may be delayed until a more suitable time could be found.

Richard, the head of geography, discussed his involvement with the Eco-Schools initiative. Eastside school had recently been awarded the prestigious Green Flag. One recent community-based initiative he had been involved with was a day event for the local community on the recycling of small electrical items.

The separate subjects (i.e. geography, history, RE) had now been combined into humanities in Key Stage 3 in Eastside school. This meant that the pupils now had eight lessons with the same teacher, rather than being spread around three different staff. This was intended to make the primary–secondary transition easier and might involve ICT in the near future as well. The effects of this new arrangement were being carefully evaluated. It was felt that, in humanities, if a teacher was teaching outside his or her pure subject specialism, with Year 7 pupils and well structured schemes of work, he or she should be able to manage the curriculum well enough.

Richard had participated in a data analysis exercise, which showed that the same children were achieving markedly different results when making comparisons of their performance in the Core subjects. The English department was regarded as the 'flagship' results-wise and it had been noted that the same pupils' performance in maths was not so good. A number of strategies had been put in place, such as interviewing heads of department, peer observations, pupil voice etc. This work had the aim of trying to tease out best practice, the outcomes being shared with the maths team to try and bring about improvement in examination results.

Katie, head of modern languages, was heavily involved in ensuring that new language courses at GCSE and A level were introduced properly, following recent revisions of the specifications. The parts of the GCSE examination concerned with reading and listening were handled externally, but now teachers were in charge of written work and speaking. The speaking element was recorded on digital recorders. The Examination Board may then select one pupil's work in every five and these pupils' work had to be recorded on to separate CDs.

It had been decided to include the film option in the curriculum for A level French. This had needed a great deal of preparation so that the pupils could answer the questions that might come up at that level.

Katie taught Welsh to other teachers in the school, to try and enhance the school's bilingual capabilities. This was one of the action points raised in the recent inspection: to raise levels of bilingualism among staff.

The school's virtual learning environment on Moodle was gradually widening its participation among the staff to enable sharing of resources to take place. Katie noted that she could spend a great deal of time uploading resources on to Moodle. The pupils could listen to a weather forecast or a newsreader reading the news in French, using Moodle-based resources. This was not seen as a major priority at the moment, in comparison to ensuring that the new examination courses were ready to be taught at the start of the academic year.

Leading The Learning: Teachers' Work with Pupils

(i) Valley Secondary School

Natasha, the deputy headteacher, explained that a great deal of work had been done with pupils in Key Stage 3 in Years 7 and 8 when teachers commented on their work using WWW (What Went Well) and EBI (Even Better If) strategies. There was some focus on curriculum continuity for Year 7 pupils with end-of-year reports including suggestions for areas they could improve on during the summer holidays.

Elizabeth, head of geography, felt it was important to try and make good use of TAs by alerting them to what was needed. A small group of pupils with learning difficulties needing additional support could then be withdrawn for extra help, to enable them to improve the quality of their learning. Lots of short, 'snappy' starters were used at the start of lessons followed by plenty of activities designed to last for suitably short periods of time. There were some concepts that were difficult to learn in geography – for example, those which applied to understanding weather and climate. Use was made of active learning strategies such as back-to-back learning, where pupils work in pairs and one describes what he or she sees on a visual image to the partner. The teacher used plenty of repetition on difficult topics by revisiting the ideas periodically.

Learning map skills and using grid references were quite challenging. To familiarize pupils with OS maps, they could be asked to plot a route home or find the grid reference for a local landmark. Another key element was making topics relevant to the pupils and taking advantage of current news items that had a geographical element: for example, teaching topics such as volcanic activity in Iceland and Montserrat; globalization in relation to global sports; and global fashion.

Pupil feedback was important as their reflections on learning and the difficulties they had encountered could help to shape the way in which a particular topic would be taught the following year.

As far as Jason, the head of maths, was concerned, the key aspects to effective learning were: (i) building a good relationship first and foremost; and (ii) making the subject relevant. Resources such as 'Maths Magic' had been used to help unlock the mysteries of algebra in an enjoyable fashion, which motivated the pupils to want to know more about how it worked.

Three key values were discussed: (i) respect, which was mutual; (ii) valuing all the answers given by pupils with no 'put downs'; (iii) curiosity, which was linked to the notion of challenge in terms of the learning goals. A great deal of emphasis was placed on AfL with the teacher asking questions to small groups of pupils and getting feedback. The use of mini-whiteboards also helped the teacher to obtain instant feedback from all the pupils. Jason did admit to the difficulties experienced in setting appropriately challenging tasks for the less-able pupils.

It was important to use carefully constructed questions to generate more thinking on the part of pupils and also to ensure that pupils could have opportunities to apply their mathematical knowledge.

(ii) Waters Edge Secondary School

Gareth, the deputy headteacher, argued that pupils leading their own learning was not only selecting activities they might do but also being reflective on their own learning, engaging with it and then deciding the next steps forward. Such an approach could only really be sustained when there was an element of real challenge involving some sort of problem-solving activity. Part of this was to allow pupils to fail to achieve their objectives and conduct some kind of evaluation, which might point out how they might do the activity more effectively next time. He mentioned one example of how a humanities teacher used a telephone directory at the start of the lesson and asked the pupils to come up with a critique of the directory, in the way that it organized information. What was interesting about this, as Gareth noted was:

> the minute they did it, teachers could see the engagement of students ... they began to get really involved in their own learning.

Building a culture of shared values and collaboration with pupils was perceived by Gareth in a very holistic fashion. Highly desirable personal values such as honesty, curiosity and integrity were accepted implicitly, without debate. However, he made some very insightful points about values, which the following extract reveals:

> the difficulty comes in taking these words [values] and making them tangible. You've got to be able to walk the walk ... and I think therefore by creating the practice in the classroom that supports those values ... so knowing every student well – there's a professional integrity there which creates a respect which allows equality and its democracy in its right sense ... You remove one and it all falls down like a pack of cards. It's the same thing in a school. You have these values at the top but if you're not living and breathing them in the classroom it isn't going to work. At the same time, you've got to create the culture where the seeds grow in the classroom and in the responses between students and teachers, it is about respect and integrity and honesty; it is about curiosity. It isn't about going in and just delivering.

Samantha (as a history teacher and progress leader for Year 8) felt that one of the most important aspects of building a shared culture with pupils was modelling the desired values and expectations for the pupils, especially at the start of the school year. That process also involved setting clear boundaries so that pupils knew what was appropriate in terms of behaviour and what their responsibilities were. However, she described the teacher's role as becoming much more facilitative. She commented that: 'it is not a done-to thing; it is a done-with thing'.

The work done in the Integrated Curriculum lessons was perceived to complement the work covered in PSHE. Marking books regularly was perceived to be a key element in the teacher knowing how well the pupils were progressing. This was significant for the quieter pupils, who would tend to 'blend in' and not be particularly vocal in the lesson. However, such pupils might be good at reflecting on their own learning.

Samantha used assessment data and benchmarking data as well as careful scrutiny of IEPs as a means by which pupils might be supported effectively to learn more effectively. Teachers carried out regular progress checks using a 1–4 system for their subject teaching where 1 meant excellent, 2 was good, 3 was sometimes unsatisfactory and 4 was a 'cause for concern'. Students who were judged to be 4 received additional support, particularly if they needed reading recovery or other appropriate interventions. Pupils evaluated how well they had worked in their teams, which gave insights into how they might improve their learning in the future. Pupils' targets were reviewed each term with their form tutor. The results were passed on to parents to make sure they were well informed about their son or daughter's progress.

Group work may mask the contributions (or lack of them) made by individual pupils. Samantha noted that:

> The conundrum is making sure that everybody is working hard and is engaged ... we always encourage teachers to set up criteria for effective group work with every individual being assigned a role which they can feedback upon.

According to Gordon (Key Stage 4 co-ordinator for English), challenge was all important, as anything that was relatively simple to learn did not lead to any real sense of achievement. Problem-solving was one of the most important skills to learn. Establishing a sense of routine and discipline was important in developing confidence in the pupils.

Monitoring exercise books was a key element to ensure the pupils achieved their potential. The pupils' own involvement in monitoring was now evident with the use of peer evaluation, self-evaluation and self-reflection. TAs played a vital role providing extra support for individuals who needed it. Employing various questioning strategies acted as a useful scaffolding tool when helping pupils to understand more difficult ideas, which allowed them to create an answer for themselves, as far as possible.

(iii) Hillside Secondary School

Sian, deputy headteacher, felt that if pupils were involved in using AfL techniques such as peer and self-assessment, this would give them every opportunity to lead their own learning. In addition, to encourage an inquisitive approach to learning, they were taught about research methods and the ways in which appropriate questions could be developed that may be particularly useful in the future. This fed into their own research, which could often be done alongside ICT. The more able and talented pupils could be challenged to set up more innovative tasks.

To be a good role model for other staff, Chris, head of PE, argued that it was important to be seen to be teaching at all levels in the school (i.e. across Key Stages 3, 4 and 5). He put a great deal of effort into ensuring that the resources (i.e. time and the necessary physical resources) were suitable and available, since PE was such a resource-rich activity. One important aspect was being able to empathize with a pupil's viewpoint, which might mean that there would be a better chance of meeting that pupil's needs. He painted a picture of the PE department as being very inclusive and this was promoted through pupils being given the opportunity to access a wide range of activities.

Creativity was perceived to be a key quality in the armoury of a teacher. A teacher can then exercise creative leadership in the sense that, as Zoe commented:

> We shape lessons for our students, taking a risk if you need to that you would have not necessarily planned when you walked in.

According to Chris, in a subject like PE a key determinant for pupils to learn effectively was differentiation: for some, this might mean making more use of visual representations, and for others, more direct instruction. He felt that targeting a weakness in a skill in a specific sport was necessary for any improvement to occur. The weakness then became a point of focus for improvement. One example might be if a pupil was struggling with physical co-ordination, it would be more co-ordination work he or she needed to concentrate on.

Zoe, head of English, considered herself to be a facilitator of learning, building a positive and conducive learning environment where individual contributions were valued. She was certainly keen on using every opportunity to 'tap into' pupils' curiosity in relation to learning:

> curiosity I like very much and taking responsibility for one's own learning and I would certainly hope that that's evident. In English we give them a lot of opportunity to do that; we value research; we value questioning as an AfL tool and as a development of self …

Although pupils liked to know where they were going on their learning journey, the pedagogical approach adopted needed to be flexible enough to pick up on their interests, especially if they were topical and relevant. For example, Zoe noted that they were fascinated by the General Election in May 2010. This had generated a lively debate among the pupils.

Helping under-achieving pupils learn effectively was Zoe's most important priority. She felt that it was important to have accurate data on each student and then to identify a suitable intervention to support each student as necessary. She placed considerable emphasis on the Learning Journals, as they could be a powerful tool for determining whether the pupils had actually understood, enjoyed and learned anything from recent lessons. Another important aspect was to see whether they could write a mark scheme for a written task, so the pupils could think about what characterized a good piece of work. Such a process was very similar to establishing what the success criteria might be for a piece of work with pupils before they started.

(iv) Eastside Secondary School

Rhodri, deputy headteacher, considered that pupils were being encouraged to lead their own learning through the adoption two or three years ago of the principles of the BLP programme (Claxton, 2002) in Year 7. This was set up by a team of dedicated Year 7 tutors who had volunteered to stay as Year 7 tutors each year. The BLP principles were aligned with the rationale for assessment for learning, particularly in relation to self-reflection on the learning process. This had helped to produce a much more questioning approach to learning; i.e. pupils posed questions themselves, which then were addressed. These could be written down and posted on so-called Learning Walls. This had been successful in the sense that pupils now had more ownership of their own learning. BLP was initially started in the local feeder primary schools and had subsequently been carried on in Eastside school. Each Year 7 class had been allocated a TA in every lesson to help address the learning needs of SEN pupils.

Richard, head of English, felt that he had shared in the building of the vision for the school. He perceived himself to be inclusive in the classroom as well as approachable and would consult on decisions as well as take them on his own, if necessary. He believed in getting the opinions of others, giving other staff responsibility and taking justifiable risks.

Building a culture of shared values and collaboration with pupils meant two distinct things: (i) inclusion, which was seen as a high priority by the headteacher; and (ii) placing the learner at the heart of the centre of everything that happened in the school. Richard used regular feedback from pupils as a way of improving learning in geography. He referred to local case studies or contexts for the subject as often as possible. 'Geography in the news' helped because there was that flexibility to tap into current global events such as the recent earthquakes in Pakistan and Haiti.

According to Richard, knowing about the learners – 'what makes them tick' – was important. A lot of emphasis was placed on good-quality marking and feedback to pupils about how they could improve their work.

The intelligent use of data was used to help pupils learn effectively. This included Fischer Family Trust information; SEN-specific data, which TAs used to help improve pupils literacy and numeracy skills; Key Stage 2 assessment information and day-to-day assessment. Challenging the pupils and being consistent as well as enthusiastic contributed to helping pupils improve the quality of their learning. Richard described 'going the extra mile' for pupils, by which he meant making sure they were enjoying the lessons, running revision classes before and after school for some pupils and producing revision booklets for the subject for GCSE pupils. The uptake of geography at GCSE was very high, alongside very large A level numbers in geography. Fieldwork and other trips out of the local area helped to bring the subject alive.

Helping EAL pupils is a high priority within Eastside School, as 20 per cent are categorized as being first language not English. These pupils' needs were addressed with help from a large number of TAs and the main ethos in the school was to immerse them in a 'sea of English'. More able and talented pupils (of which there were about 20 in each year group) experienced a curriculum enrichment programme, which was gradually being developed within the school.

Katie (head of MFL) felt that she had built a culture of shared values with the pupils by engaging in a variety of activities designed to promote positive attitudes towards the subject, for example, meeting and greeting pupils as they entered the modern languages corridor; rewarding pupils for their efforts using merits and certificates, which the pupils in Key Stage 3 could take home; being friendly and approachable; and using YouTube for stimulating visual resources in lessons. She commented that:

> When you teach students, they have to be secure in the fact that you will do your best for them ... I do try and instill a feeling of 'You can do this.' You might need a second explanation, but you will get there: just keep at it.

Katie perceived routine to be important so that pupils knew where they were in terms of behaviour. Educational trips abroad were seen to be important in terms of developing pupils' language skills, as was the constant upgrading of classroom resources to be used in lessons.

Having learning partners as part of paired work was one thing that Katie thought was important for pupils. It meant that if anyone needed help, he or she could consult his or her partner.

A recent change had occurred as a result of discovering that some pupils were not choosing to study a language to GCSE level because of perceived grammar difficulties. On investigation, it was discovered that they were finding the past tense quite difficult to comprehend, so it was now referred to rather more superficially in Year 9 and then revisited in more depth in Years 10 and 11 when the pupils were more mature.

Thinking skills were emphasized in some French lessons where, for example, pupils were asked to decide which was the odd one out in a set of colours: e.g. red, blue and green. There was no right answer, and any type of answer was likely to be correct. However, it was the thinking process that was important, because the pupils had to explain their answer and give their reasons.

With SEN pupils, Katie commented that if pupils were struggling with poor communication skills in English as 'baggage' from primary school, then at least they could come along to French lessons and start with another language from scratch.

Teacher Collaboration with Other Teachers and Support Staff

(i) Valley Secondary School

Collaboration with geography teachers in other schools was perceived by Elizabeth, head of geography, to be desirable and mutually beneficial as part of an online learning community/discussion group to share resources and ideas. Regular fortnightly meetings were scheduled on the timetable to allow staff to meet together. Every half term one meeting also occurred after school. There was a great deal of informal sharing occurring, as teaching rooms were located next to each other. Effective work was done with other staff when organizing and running annual fieldwork. This took place in a national park and meant that pupils walked the length of a river from source to mouth. This piece of work contributed 10 per cent towards the pupils' GCSE grades.

According to Jason, head of maths, informal discussion played a key role in helping to achieve some degree of departmental consistency. With three full-time and six part-time members, it was difficult to keep in touch with them all. E-mail messages helped, but not all the staff read them regularly. With the part-time staff, teaching maths was not their number-one priority, even though they would not be likely to let the pupils down in any way. There were very occasional meetings arranged during the school day to allow the head of maths to speak to all the staff teaching the subject.

Several barriers to teacher collaboration were mentioned by Natasha, the deputy headteacher, including: (i) time constraints, which had been exacerbated by the newly introduced 'rarely cover' arrangements; (ii) internal pressure to compare results across subjects within school; and (iii) externally driven pressure to compare results across the local authority.

However, greater collaboration could occur in two ways:

- Placing staff in small groups with other staff with whom they had not worked before;
- Using a voluntary working lunch system to bring staff together to consider a specific topic and then discuss it.

(ii) Waters Edge Secondary School

Samantha (history and progress leader for Year 8) described the composition of her team of nine form tutors as all being experienced teachers within the school. With the introduction of the Integrated Curriculum, she wanted to work with experienced staff who knew the values and ethos of the school. With them, she had been able to create schemes of work, lesson plans and resources that were produced collaboratively and of which staff had ownership. The team of tutors met regularly once a week after school. Two staff members were initially anxious about pupils doing extended pieces of written work because they would not usually do such work as part of their day-to-day teaching. A great deal of support was forthcoming from an English teacher and the head of history to provide help with sentence starters, writing frames etc. Samantha noted that as Year 7 tutors they would know their pupils very well by the end of the year, as they would have worked with them for four hours a fortnight. She made reference to the importance of providing pupils with a rigorous learning experience. She thought it would take about five years for all the staff to gain sufficient experience as form tutors working within the Integrated Curriculum to gain the full benefits from it.

Gordon (Key Stage 4 co-ordinator in English) argued that the culture of shared values and collaboration in his department was built around meeting together regularly, pooling ideas, monitoring and observations of each other's lessons. He also worked in the Welsh department, trying to promote bilingualism. He had co-hosted the Eisteddfod with the head of the Welsh department, which again promoted collaboration between staff.

Gareth, deputy headteacher, felt that the school environment (i.e. the design of the buildings and the classrooms themselves) did not necessarily help promote teacher collaboration. He argued that greater teacher collaboration would only occur when 'there are more multi-purpose learning spaces with technology to support it'.

(iii) Hillside Secondary School

From Sian's perspective as deputy headteacher, many teachers were willing to be involved with developing relatively new ideas, and among those currently operating in the school were Building Learning Power (BLP), Assessment for learning (AfL), the Welsh Baccalaureate and Essential (or Key) Skills. Some job shadowing (e.g. with heads of year) was encouraged for staff development purposes. This was perceived to be an opportunity for those who wished to take advantage of it. Some staff were willing to take on more responsibilities, but only if they received some additional financial remuneration for it, which was not available in the current economic climate.

Sian was of the opinion that there was too little cross-departmental co-operation and too few cross-curricular links being made. This was mainly due to workload issues and the pressures generated by the examination system in Key Stage 4. However, she felt that there was increasing amounts of cross-curricular work going on in Key Stage 3, with more recent emphasis on skills development, especially on a day that was organized with a re-arranged timetable.

In the English department Zoe worked to build a culture of shared values and collaboration within a large department (of twelve staff in total).She felt that this was based on formal and informal dialogue, with informal contact being crucial to encouraging others staff and troubleshooting. Such informal contacts occurred in corridors, the staff room, after school etc. The core departmental value concerned notions of supporting each other and teamwork. There was plenty of delegation of responsibilities within the English department.

One new approach being developed with Year 9 pupils was for them to achieve Level 2 in 'Communication' by the end of the year, to minimize any tension between English as a subject and communication as a key skill.

Involving support staff in the planning for devising lessons with SEN pupils was extremely important. Usually, the TA knew individual SEN pupils well and was well aware of their individual learning needs. In fact, it may be that the TA's influence on the child's learning was possibly greater than that of the teacher, although this view would not be supported by the research findings reported by Webster et al. (2011).

Teacher collaboration was perceived by Chris (head of PE) as being extremely important for this subject at Hillside school. This started with the recruitment process, where the selection of an individual depended as much as anything else on that person identifying strongly with the core values being promoted with PE. Technical expertise was insufficient. In PE, a great deal of work was done collaboratively with colleagues, and normally three staff members of each gender were teaching at the same time. In a mixed GCSE class, a male and female teacher worked alongside each other. In A level PE, a more senior member of staff could work along a much less-experienced colleague.

One of the more unusual approaches that had been adopted was the use of the least experienced staff being mentors for trainee PE teachers. Chris defended such an approach for two reasons:

> First of all, they have a greater empathy with a trainee and secondly, they are more up to speed with the actual requirements of the teacher training course … In addition, having to mentor someone else is a phenomenal piece of professional development.

Time was always a barrier to teacher collaboration, which could only really occur outside normal lesson times such as before or after school. Additionally, a lack of appropriate resources was thought to hinder collaboration. The newly introduced policy of 'rarely cover' was having a rather negative impact on some extra-curricular activities. However, there was plenty of cross-curricular co-operation in the school, for example the new humanities course in Year 7 and key skills being certificated in Year 9 with the help of the geography and RE departments.

(iv) Eastside Secondary School

Richard had been head of department in geography for five years. He commented that he would not ask anybody to do anything that he would not do. A great deal of collaborative effort had gone in to getting the new humanities course up and running, as more non-specialists were now teaching geography in Key Stage 3.

Working in Partnership with Parents

(i) Valley Secondary School

A great deal of faith appeared to be placed in the constructive use of pupils' planners. Space was available for parents to comment on their child's progress. Other ways of supporting learning included sending home certificates of achievement on an individual basis, and the geography department also used postcards to congratulate pupils on their achievements.

(ii) Waters Edge Secondary School

Here there was a variety of traditional communication mechanisms such as parents evenings, comments in the pupils' planners, school reports etc., but some parents offered work experience placements to pupils as well.

Phone clinics were used whereby the form tutor contacted the parents to discuss their child's academic progress (but not for behaviour). The use of the child's planner was seen as a good way of getting feedback, especially to celebrate any achievements that occurred outside of school. When parents toured the school as part of the Key Stage 2–3 transition process, they might observe five to ten minutes of a lesson.

(iii) Hillside Secondary School

Zoe (head of English) commented that parents often rang up and asked for advice about ways of getting their son or daughter interested in reading. They also responded well if they were contacted about missing coursework. One way of sending out positive messages to parents in Hillside school was through the staging of an annual event called the Year 11 Anthology evening, where pupils showcased their literary efforts. Parents were invited in to witness the students perform their writing, read extracts, and sometimes use music or drama. This event had been very well attended and the effort put in was appreciated by the parents.

One other useful point of contact with parents occurred when the English staff held a workshop event after school to discuss ways of assisting parents to help their son or daughter revise for examinations. They were also shown how to help pupils with a revision booklet.

(iv) Eastside Secondary School

The deputy headteacher referred to an external agency that had been employed in recent years to conduct surveys with the parents, to ask questions about curriculum issues and anti-bullying and homework policies, which the parents had responded to anonymously. Feedback on regular reports and homework planners were also methods by which parental views could be expressed.

What Does This Evidence Indicate About Teachers Taking Responsibility for Teaching and Learning?

(i) Support for teacher leadership

General support from the SLT was noted for teacher leadership in all the schools visited (Durrant and Holden, 2006), but it was found that in Valley school, financial difficulties had tended to restrict participation in decision-making. However, all the schools indicated that staff were involved in the decision-making process to some degree. 'Pupil voice' was apparent in all the schools (i.e. they all had school councils and some schools were involving pupils in the selection of new members of staff). However, the teacher leadership perspective should not ignore ideas about pupil leadership. In practice, this would mean pupils becoming more independent as learners, directly influencing what and how they might learn.

(ii) School improvement

To develop and maintain school improvement, a wide range of initiatives were embraced in the schools visited, including the Welsh Baccalaureate, Building Learning Power (Claxton, 2002), Eco-Schools, sport for recreation and internal monitoring of standards across subject departments, although many of the government-funded initiatives in England were not available in Wales. All of the teacher-leaders interviewed were leading change to a greater or lesser degree in their main areas of influence (Durrant and Holden, 2006).

There was general encouragement to be actively involved in initiatives, but teachers were usually expected to use the line management system as a 'filter' (Harris and Muijs, 2005). It was also noted that in Waters Edge School the emphasis in Key Stage 3 was on skills development, which had been driven by policy changes introduced by the Welsh Assembly Government (DCELLS, 2008b). This had led to the introduction of the 'Integrated Curriculum', where the main emphasis was on the development of cross-curricular skills, such as problem-solving and extended writing.

(iii) Teacher-leaders working with pupils

As regards building a culture of shared values and collaboration with pupils, the promotion of key values was perceived very positively by teacher-leaders. These included honesty, integrity, respect, curiosity, tolerance and community awareness. These were not regarded as being mutually exclusive but quite the opposite: closely interconnected. Translating them into the 'lived' practice in the classroom presented staff with the challenge of being able to model them in a consistent fashion.

Setting clear expectations and boundaries both in terms of behaviour and attitudes to learning were deemed by many of those interviewed to be vital.

In several of the schools visited, inclusion was a high priority. In Eastside school, Richard, head of geography, highlighted the need to know the learners, i.e. 'what makes them tick'.

Other aspects of working with pupils included the facilitation role of the teacher, which was in evidence as pupils could be encouraged to lead their own learning, and this was a common thread running through the responses of those interviewed. This had several elements, including developing pupils' metacognitive abilities (McGregor, 2007 and Loughran, 2010) by building in time to reflect upon their own learning and the promotion of open-ended problem-solving activities with an appropriate level of challenge (Muijs and Reynolds, 2005).

Many of the teacher-leaders interviewed mentioned the use of AfL techniques (Black and Wiliam, 1998) such as monitoring, questioning and self-evaluation as being effective.

Several staff mentioned the use of TAs to help SEN pupils and noted the difficulty in setting work at the right level for SEN pupils in subjects like maths.

A number of teacher-leaders noted the use of various types of assessment data, including benchmarking data, Fischer Family Trust information and Key Stage 2 data to help promote pupils' learning.

(iv) Teacher-leaders working collaboratively with other staff

There was evidence of teacher collaboration in all the schools visited, giving staff the opportunity to engage in professional dialogue and discussion (Harris and Muijs, 2005). Traditional forms of communication in meetings were mentioned when considering collaboration with staff. Jason, head of maths in Valley school, noted the difficulties in maintaining regular communication with a mix of full-time and part-time staff. There was some evidence of growing forms of teacher collaboration in connection with sharing resources and ideas with teachers in other schools as part of an online community.

The nature of some subjects required more collaboration, for example PE. Shared values and collaboration among staff occurred in both formal and informal contacts between staff.

Various barriers to collaboration mentioned including lack of time, accountability (e.g. internal pressures to compare subject performance across departments and external pressure from the local authority to compare results across schools) and lack of resources (Harris and Muijs, 2005).

(v) Teachers working with parents

Communication with parents via traditional means such as phone calls, school reports and pupil planners was regarded as very important in all the schools. It was also perceived to be important to celebrate pupils' achievement at every opportunity.

11 Conclusions

Introduction

The research described in this book provides a snapshot to illustrate some of the issues currently associated with the work of teacher-leaders. It has given an opportunity for a sample of teachers to have a 'voice'; to explain what they do to promote pupils' learning whilst working in different contexts. Teacher leadership is an inclusive concept as it is not just restricted to those with formally designated responsibilities or those in receipt of a TLR. Durrant and Holden (2006) argued that 'Teacher leadership need not be tied to particular roles, tasks or status; it is a dimension of all teachers' professionalism' (p.31). It has been conceptualized as having two key dimensions:

- leading the learning in the classroom with pupils and TAs and
- collaboration with colleagues outside the classroom.

The degree of influence exerted by a teacher-leader on colleagues is difficult to investigate fully. As was discussed in Chapter 2, some colleagues may be more easily influenced than others. It has to be acknowledged that a given teacher may be influenced by other colleagues (e.g. in terms of attitudes or behaviour) without consciously realizing the degree to which he or she is being influenced. In addition, teachers tend to work with small groups of colleagues (subject departments in secondary schools or year groups in primary schools), so there is the influence of a group to consider as well (i.e. conforming to group norms and behaviour), although this aspect was not part of the research carried out for this book.

When considering the teacher-leaders' responses from different national perspectives (i.e. England and Wales), far fewer major *differences* emerged than was anticipated. This was particularly true when considering the teachers' responses to questions about leading the learning in the classroom and collaborating with other colleagues. Those differences that did emerge appeared to reflect those that exist mainly at the *policy level*. There are different curriculum arrangements in Wales compared to England. In England, there was more reference to and emphasis placed on personalized learning by those teacher-leaders interviewed, while in Wales the development of skills was perceived to be a high priority, reflecting current government policy. The development of the Welsh language among both pupils and teachers was deemed to be important for several teacher-leaders interviewed.

Until May 2010, primary and secondary schools in England had access to a wide range of government-funded initiatives. These were mainly targeted at raising children's attainment in literacy and numeracy, where there was evidence of under-achievement. However, these funded interventions were generally not available in Wales. There is some evidence that they achieved a measure of success in the short term but without the additional funding could not be sustained. Following the election of the coalition government, the funding for these interventions was been withdrawn. However, concerns about standards in literacy and numeracy remain, particularly in the light of the recently published PISA (2009) results.

The interview data showed that there were many *similarities* between the perceptions of teacher-leaders in schools in England and Wales. All the members of the SLTs in the schools visited indicated in one way or another that leadership was distributed in their school. The extent to which it was distributed varied from one school to another. However, the asymmetrical power relationships referred to by Busher (2006) were still in evidence as most of the members of the SLT interviewed tended to discuss such forms of distribution in the formal organizational framework and, as would be expected, retained the power to consent or decline any school improvement initiatives that might be suggested by staff.

Whilst there was some involvement in decision-making at the whole school level, it was much more apparent at the classroom level, when teacher-leaders were able to artic-ulate how they consulted pupils on their learning and worked closely with TAs to decide the most appropriate ways of supporting the learning of SEN pupils. There was plenty of evidence that listening to the *learner voice* was becoming more important through the use of surveys and giving pupils time to reflect on their own learning.

Teacher-leaders Leading The Learning in The Classroom

General findings

It should be borne in mind that a case study approach using teacher-leaders working in a wide variety of different contexts does make any form of generalization difficult. That said, a number of points can be made about recurring themes that emerged from the interview data.

O'Donoghue and Clarke (2010) cited Harris and Muijs (2005) when discussing what leading the learning might mean. They argued that this is 'continuing to teach and improve individual teaching proficiency' (p.92). In this research, the teacher-leaders noted the importance of *differentiating the level of the task* so that it included an appropriate level of challenge for each pupil. Many of those interviewed mentioned the beneficial effects of using assessment for learning techniques with pupils, including monitoring progress using different questioning strategies, peer and self-assessment.

Bearing in mind the emphasis on accountability and the target-driven education policies pursued by the previous government, it is hardly surprising that there was some evidence, especially from teacher-leaders working in England, that pupils' progress was being tracked very carefully using systems such as APP. The coalition government has distanced itself to some extent from the prescriptive use of the APP system (DfE, 2010).

It was found that many of the teacher-leaders interviewed encouraged pupils to engage in *self-reflection* and *metacognitive processes* such as 'Learning to Learn' or 'Building Learning Power' (Claxton, 2002). This helped to generate more of ownership of their learning among pupils. The staff themselves were very aware of the need to *model desirable moral values* such as honesty, showing respect for others etc. in the classroom.

A number of the schools visited contained pupils from very diverse backgrounds. The prevailing culture of acceptance and inclusion dominated the discourse about teaching and learning in those schools.

In both England and Wales, there has been more emphasis on *skills development* in the last three or four years, as discussed in Chapter 4. However, this was particularly evident in Wales following the publication of the Skills Framework document (DCELLS, 2008b) by the Welsh Assembly Government. The nearest direct equivalent of this document in England is the one produced by QCDA in 2009. This was evident in the recent introduction of a more skills-based approach to learning (e.g. the 'Integrated Curriculum' in Waters Edge Secondary School in Wales and the 'Skills for Life' approach adopted in Manor Primary School in England).

The *role of the teacher* has slowly changed under the weight of recent policy reforms and changes to the inspection framework. This can be summed up as a change from the teacher directing the learning and the pupils being regarded as passive learners to the teacher facilitating learning with the pupils themselves making more active decisions about what and how they might learn. A number of the teacher-leaders interviewed discussed their aims for pupils to become more independent in their approach to learning and the teacher to guide this process through discussion and consultation as appropriate.

For any given classroom-based activity, there will always be a balance between the pupils' control over their own learning and the teacher's control. The proportions will vary according to the age and ability of the pupils. However, the pupil's learning can never be totally *independent* of the teacher, as the teacher does retain the overall responsibility for progression and outcomes in terms of pupils' learning. Figure 11.1 illustrates this change in the role of the teacher. The right-hand column summarizes what pupil leadership might actually mean in practice.

Teacher in Control of Pupils' Learning	Teacher as Facilitator of Learning; Pupils have More Control of their Own Learning
Teacher active; pupils passive recipients of knowledge	Pupils actively involved in their own learning; e.g. researching, investigating, discussing etc.
Pupils very dependent on the teacher	Pupils have more ownership of their own learning. It becomes more personalized.
Teacher as 'Learning Director'	Teacher as 'Learning Consultant'
Whole class teaching is the dominant strategy used	Individual or small group work is much in evidence
Teacher decides how a task will be tackled	Pupils decide how a task will be tackled and how they will present their findings. Teacher consulted as necessary

Fig. 11.1 Comparing two contrasting conceptualizations of the teacher's role in pupils' learning

There was evidence from teacher-leaders' comments of greater emphasis being placed on developing pupils' collaborative skills to be used in small group work. This reflected a desire, on the part of teacher-leaders, to see teams of pupils working more effectively, nurturing a sense of *interdependence*.

All the teachers interviewed were more than happy to describe themselves as *learners*. This would be made clear to the pupils and the notion of 'teacher as learner' was especially powerful in the context of building a culture of shared values.

Context-Specific Findings

In primary schools in England and Wales there were six key findings in relation to leading the learning in the classroom:

1 According to some teacher-leaders, certain aspects of the primary curriculum, especially maths, required more whole class teaching.
2 One teacher-leader referred to the effectiveness of the 'closing the gap' approach (DfES, 2007) to marking pupils' work where the teacher poses a questions or questions that the pupil can then address and thereby create a dialogue in terms of helping pupils' learning to progress.
3 More use of open-ended questioning techniques was advocated as a way of developing children's thinking skills.
4 The use of success criteria was noted by some teacher-leaders as a way of clarifying how pupils might improve the quality of their written work.
5 The use of skill ladders (e.g. for self-assessment purposes) was found to be useful to improve

group work participation. These skills include collaborating with others; listening to other pupils' opinions etc.

6 Celebrating achievement appeared to be used extensively in the schools visited, as an important aspect of leading the learning to sustain the motivation of learners.

In secondary schools in England and Wales there were three key findings in relation to leading the learning as a result of the interviews with teacher-leaders:

1 The importance of challenge was noted through the use of different types of problem-solving activities. There was also reference made to the need for more innovative tasks for the able and talented pupils.

2 Self-evaluation was considered to be a very important aspect in the sense that pupils needed to have the opportunity to reflect upon their own learning and develop their metacognitive abilities. Zoe (head of English in Hillside school) mentioned the value of 'learning journals' to help with this process.

3 Pupils' learning was enhanced when they knew more about the different kinds of research methods that could be employed to gather data, which might help answer their own questions.

Teacher-Leaders Collaborating with Their Colleagues

General findings

Formal meetings of staff (i.e. in a given Year group in primary school or in a subject department in secondary school) were held regularly to discuss curriculum development or strategies that might be used to tackle pupil under-achievement. Such meetings can help to create a positive learning climate where reflective enquiry takes place on a regular basis. This can help to translate often unspoken or tacit knowledge into shared knowledge and thus generate new ideas to solve problems (Earley and Bubb, 2004). Developing curriculum knowledge is a key feature of teacher leadership (O'Donoghue and Clarke, 2010). Several teacher-leaders mentioned the usefulness of *informal contacts* between staff outside regular meetings, which could occur in or out of school. As a corollary to the previous point, there was some evidence for the notion that teacher-leaders offer plenty of support to other teachers in the form of guidance when using innovative teaching strategies. Wenger (1998) argued that mutual engagement was an important aspect of developing a community of practice. *Positive working relationships* with other staff were a key feature as a pre-condition for any meaningful collaboration. There was a great deal of value placed on *teamwork* among staff who shared a common responsibility; i.e. taught the same subject or in the same Key Stage.

Context-specific findings

In primary schools in England and Wales there were four key findings in relation to working with colleagues:

(i) Staff were able to collaborate when discussing the work of a specific year group or, as in the case of Manor Primary School, if they were part of team of teachers responsible for a group of subjects across the whole school. There was some discussion among staff about how to help under-achieving pupils improve, in terms of their learning. This is a form of collaborative action planning highlighted by O'Donoghue and Clarke (2010) as part of what teacher-leaders actually do.

(ii) The 'lesson study' initiative in Galaxy Primary School appeared to be a very useful professional development tool as a way of studying the processes of learning by observing pupils in class and then interviewing them afterwards and giving the pupils themselves an opportunity to reflect upon their own learning.

(iii) Collaboration between staff could be problematic, either through a lack of time, finance or split classes. It was difficult to arrange PPA time so that staff could work together during the school day. Any staff time together that did occur was fitted in after school. However, one school (Central Primary School) was able to arrange one half-day a week for staff to meet together. Where a mixed year group had been created, time had to be devoted to ensuring that there was no repetition of tasks or activities.

(iv) There was some evidence that TAs would stay with particular pupils and get to know their strengths and weaknesses very well during the course of the school year. The TAs would be allocated to a specific class and could be used to help develop the literacy and numeracy skills of SEN pupils in particular.

In secondary schools in England and Wales there were seven key findings that emerged in relation to working with colleagues:

(i) Working closely with TAs, when preparing and delivering lessons for SEN and EAL pupils, was regarded as being very important.

(ii) Close collaboration among the staff working within a specific subject area like PE was essential. Chris (head of PE in Hillside school) noted the importance of all the PE staff aligning themselves with the core values of the department. He advocated the use of less-experienced staff mentoring trainee teachers. Coaching and mentoring can play a key role in developing teacher leadership in schools. It is one of the key features of teacher leadership, according to O'Donoghue and Clarke (2010).

(iii) Coaching and mentoring may be viewed as being couched in terms of a 'novice–expert' relationship, i.e. a one-to-one relationship between two teachers where good interpersonal skills are very important. There is considerable overlap in terms of meaning between the concepts of coaching and mentoring. Coaching is normally perceived to be more of a skills-based process while mentoring may involve more counselling.

(iv) An alternative form of collaboration that relates to the development of the curriculum was highlighted by Elizabeth, working as head of geography in Valley school. She advocated the benefits of collaborating with subject teachers in other schools as part of an online community, especially in relation to sharing resources.

(v) In Grange school the headteacher had given the responsibility for helping to raise standards of teaching and learning to effective teachers in a subject area outside their own specialisms. This was recognized as being a challenging task and required diplomacy, professional judgement and patience on the part of the designated teacher-leader.

(vi) Taking responsibility for teaching and learning with colleagues for Jill in Beehive school meant working with a number of colleagues on developing a whole school approach to assessment for learning. However, this had proved somewhat problematic, as the implementation of such a policy was not found to be universal. Paul, in Beehive school, noted the use of learning walks with the head of department or person formally responsible for teaching and learning in a given subject area to observe classroom practice.

(viii) Any barriers to collaboration between staff were mainly due to time constraints, internal pressure to compare the performance of pupils across different subject areas and external pressure to compare the performance of schools with a given local authority. The external pressure on schools remains with the publication of 'families of schools' data featuring similar schools in a given region as, inevitably, comparisons will be made between schools on the performance of their pupils. There were examples given of the communication problems that arise when some senior staff teach part-time in a subject area and have other whole school responsibilities.

Working with parents

Many of the more traditional means of communicating with parents were mentioned (e.g. reports, parents' evenings) as well as texting parents to remind them about anything their child might need to bring to school that day or the next day or phoning parents when there might an issue in relation to possible under-achievement. The importance of regular communication and the open-door policy were highly valued by all the teacher-leaders working in the primary sector.

Final Comment

The picture painted in this book of the work of teacher-leaders is far from complete. However, one of the recurring themes has been about partnership: between teachers and pupils, teachers and other teachers, teachers and TAs, and teachers and parents. The nature and full potential of the benefits of these collaborative partnerships to promote pupils' learning has yet to be fully explored, but it is to be hoped that this book has made a useful contribution to understanding them in the context of primary and secondary schools in England and Wales.

References

Adey, P., Robertson, A. and Venville, G. (2001) *Let's Think! A programme for developing thinking in five and six year olds: teacher's guide*, Windsor, NFER-Nelson

Atkinson, T. and Claxton, G. (2000) *The Intuitive Practitioner*, Buckingham, Open University Press

Ausubel, D. (1968) *Educational Psychology: A cognitive view*, New York, Holt, Rinehart and Winston

Bacharach, S. (1988) 'Notes on a political theory of educational organisations' in A. Westoby, *Culture and Power in Educational Organisations*, Milton Keynes, Open University Press

Bandura, A. (1995) *Self-Efficacy in Changing Societies*, Cambridge, Cambridge University Press

Black, P. and Wiliam, D. (1998) *Inside the Black Box*, London, King's College, London

Blasé, J. and Anderson, G. (1995) *The Micropolitics of Educational Leadership: From control to empowerment*, London: Cassell

Blatchford, P., Bassett, P., Brown, P. and Webster, R. (2009) 'The effect of support staff on pupil engagement and individual attention', *British Educational Research Journal* 35, 5: 661–86

Bolman, L.G. and Deal, T.E. (1994) 'Looking for leadership: another search party's report', *Educational Administration Quarterly* 30, 1: 77–96.

Bowring-Carr, C. and West-Burnham, J. (1997) *Effective Learning in Schools*, London, Financial Times, Pitman

British Education Research Council (BERA) (2004) Revised Ethical Guidelines for Educational Research, http://www.bera.ac.uk/files/guidelines/ethica1.pdf (accessed 16 August 2010)

Busher, H. (2006) *Understanding Educational Leadership: People power and culture*, Maidenhead, Open University Press

Bush, T. and Glover, D. (2003) School Leadership: Concepts and evidence http://www.mp.gov.rs/resursi/dokumenti/dok217-eng-School_Leadership_Concepts_and_Evidence.pdf (accessed 12 August 2010)

Chrispeels, J. (2004) *Learning to Lead Together: The promise and challenge of sharing leadership*, London, Sage

Claxton, G.L. (1997) *Hare Brain, Tortoise Mind: Why intelligence increases when you think less*, London, Fourth Estate

Claxton, G.L. (2002) *Building Learning Power*, Bristol, TLO

Close, P. and Raynor, A. (2010) 'Five literatures of organisation: putting the context back into educational leadership', *School Leadership and Management*, 30, 3: 209–24

Cohen, L., Manion, L. and Morrison, K. (2007) *Research Methods in Education*, London, Routledge

Day, C. and Harris, A. (2003) 'Teacher leadership, reflective practice and school improvement' in K. Leithwood and P. Hallinger (eds) *Second International Handbook of Educational Leadership and Administration*, Dordrecht, Kluwer Academic

DCELLS (2008a) *Making the Most of Learning: Implementing the revised curriculum*, Cardiff, WAG

DCELLS (2008b) *Skills Framework for 3 to 19 Year Olds in Wales*, Cardiff, WAG.

DCELLS (2008c) *Framework for Children's Learning for 3–7 Year Olds in Wales*, Cardiff, WAG

DCELLS (2008d) *School Effectiveness Framework: building effective learning communities together*, Cardiff, WAG

DCELLS (2009) *Foundation Phase Child Development Profile Guidance*, Cardiff, WAG

DCSF (2007) *The Children's Plan: Building brighter futures*, available at http://www.dcsf.gov.uk/childrensplan/ (accessed 25 March 2010)

DCSF(2008) *Improving Practice and Progression through Lesson Study*, http://nationalstrategies.standards.dcsf.gov.uk/node/132730 (accessed 15 September 2010)

DCSF (2009) *Independent Review of the Primary Curriculum: Final report (Rose review)* http://www.

education.gov.uk/publications/standard/publicationdetail/page1/DCSF-00499-2009 (accessed 23 March 2011)

DCSF (2010) *Assessing Pupils' Progress: A teacher's handbook*, http://nationalstrategies.standards.dcsf.gov.uk/ (accessed 29 July 2010)

DES (1988) *Advancing A Levels: Report of a committee chaired by Professor G. Higginson (The Higginson Report)*, London: HMSO

DfE (2010) The Importance of Teaching: The Schools White Paper 2010, http://www.education.gov.uk/publications/eOrderingDownload/CM-7980.pdf (accessed 26 April 2011)

DfE (2011) Approved Free School Proposals http://www.education.gov.uk/schools/leadership/typesofschools/freeschools/b0066077/free-school-proposals/ (accessed 3 March 2011)

DfES (2003) *Raising Standards and Tackling Workload: A national agreement* http://www.tda.gov.uk/upload/resources/na_standards_workload.pdf (accessed 29 July 2010)

DfES (2004) *The Children's Act*, http://www.dcsf.gov.uk/childrenactreport/ (accessed 29 July 2010)

DfES (2005) *School Improvement: Lessons from research*, available on http://www.innovationunit.org/images/stories/files/pdf/school_improvement.pdf (accessed 12 August 2010)

DfES (2007) *2020 Vision: Report of the Teaching and Learning in 2020 Review Group*, http://publications.education.gov.uk/eOrderingDownload/6856-DfES-Teaching%20and%20Learning.pdf (accessed 29 July 2010)

Dimmock, C. (2000) *Designing the Learning-Centred School: A cross-cultural perspective*, London, Falmer Press

DuFour, R. (2004) 'What is a "professional learning community"? *Educational Leadership* June 2004: 61, 8, p. 6–11.

Durrant, J. and Holden, G. (2006) *Teachers Leading Change: Doing research for school improvement*, London, Paul Chapman

Earley, P. and Bubb, S. (2004) *Leading and Managing Continuing Professional Development*, London, Paul Chapman

Edmond, N. and Price, M. (2009) 'Workforce remodelling and pastoral care in schools: a diversification of roles or a de-professionalisation of functions?' *Pastoral Care in Education*, 27, 4, December 2009: 301–11

Eraut, M. (1994) *Developing Professional Knowledge and Competence*, London, Falmer Press

Eraut, M. (2000) 'Non-formal learning, implicit learning and tacit knowledge in professional work' in F. Coffield (ed.) *The Necessity of Informal Learning*, Bristol, The Policy Press

Eraut, M. (2004) 'Informal learning in the workplace', *Studies in Continuing Education* 26, 2: 247–73

Fitzgerald, T. and Gunter, H. (2008) 'Contesting the orthodoxy of teacher leadership', *School Leadership and Management*, 11, 4: 331–40

Flutter J. and Ruddock, J. (2004) *Consulting Pupils: What's in it for schools*, London, RoutledgeFalmer

Frost, D. and Durrant, J. (2003) 'Teacher leadership: rationale, strategy and impact', *School Leadership and Management* 23, 2: 173–86

Fullan, M. (1991) *The New Meaning of Educational Change*, London, Cassell.

Fullan, M. (1997) 'Planning, doing and coping with change' in A. Harris, N. Bennett and M. Preedy, *Organisational Effectiveness and Improvement in Education*, Buckingham, Open University Press

Fullan, M. (ed.) (2009) *The Challenge of Change: Start school improvement now!* Thousand Oaks, CA, Corwin

Gleeson, D. and Gunter, H. (2001) 'The performing school and the modernisation of teachers' in *The Performing School: managing, teaching and learning in a performance culture*, London, RoutledgeFalmer

Gleeson, D. and Keep, E. (2004) 'Voice without accountability: the changing relationship between employers, the state and education in England', *Oxford Review of Education* 30, 1, March 2004: 37–63

Glover, D. and Law, S. (2002) *Improving Learning: Professional practice in secondary schools*, Buckingham, Open University Press

Gray, J. (2005) 'Three tough issues for long-term school improvement' in DfES, *School Improvement – Lessons from research*, available on http://www.innovationunit.org/images/stories/files/pdf/school_improvement.pdf (accessed 12 August 2010)

Gronn, P. (2003) *The New Work of Educational Leaders: Changing leadership practice in an era of school reform*, London, Chapman

Gunter, H. (2005) *Leading Teachers*, London, Continuum

Guskey, T.R. (2002) 'Professional development and change', *Teachers and Teaching: Theory and Practice* 8, 3/4: 381–91

Hacker, D.J. (1998) Chapter 1: 'Definitions and empirical foundations' in D. Hacker, J. Dunlosky and A. Graesser (eds) *Metacognition in Educational Theory and Practice*, New Jersey, Lawrence Erlbaum

Hargreaves, D. (2001) 'A capital theory of school effectiveness and improvement', *British Educational Research Journal* 27, 4: 487–503

Harris, A. and Muijs, D. (2005) *Improving Schools through Teacher Leadership*, Maidenhead, Open University Press

Harris, A. (2003) 'Teacher leadership as distributed leadership: heresy, fantasy or possibility?' *School Leadership and Management* 23, 3: 313–24

Harris, A. and Lambert, L. (2003) *Building Leadership Capacity for School Improvement*, Maidenhead, Open University Press

Harris, B. (2004) 'Leading by Heart', *School Leadership and Management* 24, 4: 391–404

Harris, B. (2007) *Supporting the Emotional Work of School Leaders*, London, Paul Chapman

Hay McBer (2000) *Research in Teacher Effectiveness: A model of teacher effectiveness*, London, DfEE

Hitchcock, G. and Hughes, D. (1995) *Research and the Teacher: A qualitative introduction to school-based research*, London, Routledge

Hodgkinson, C. (1991) *Educational Leadership: The moral art*, New York, State University of New York Press

Holmes, B., Tangey, B., Fitzgibbon, A., Savage, T. and Meehan, S. (2001) 'Communal constructivism: students constructing learning for as well as with others' in J. Price, D. Willis, N.E. Davis and J. Willis (eds) *Proceedings of the 12th International Conference of the Society for Information Technology and Teacher Education* (SITE 2001) pp.3114–3119, Chesapeake, VA.

Holmes, B. and Gardner, J. (2006) *E-Learning: Concepts and practice*, London, Sage

Hopkins, D. and Harris, A. (1997) 'Improving the quality of education for all', *Support for Learning* 12, 4: 147–51

Hoyle, E. (1986) *The Politics of School Management*, London, Hodder & Stoughton

Hoyle, E. and Wallace, M. (2005) *Educational Leadership: Ambiguity, Professionals and Managerialism*, London, Sage

Hughes, M. (2002) *Tweak to Transform*, Stafford, Network Educational Press.

Hurley, L. (2002) 'The challenge of parental involvement' in M. Cole (ed.) *Professional Values and Practice for Teachers and Student Teachers*, London, David Fulton

lleris, K. (2007) *How We learn: Learning and non-learning in school and beyond*, London, Routledge

Jones, C. and Pound, L. (2008) *Leadership and Management in the Early Years*, Maidenhead, Open University Press

Jordan, A., Carille, O. and Stack, A. (2008) *Approaches to Learning: A guide for teachers*, Maidenhead, Open University Press

Katzenmeyer, M. and Moller, G. (2001) *Awakening the Sleeping Giant: Helping teachers develop as leaders,* Thousand Oaks, CA, Corwin Press

Kolb, D. (1984) *Experiential Learning*, Englewood Cliffs, NJ, Prentice Hall

Leicester Mercury (2010) 'School leavers not up to work', Tuesday 15 June 2010

Leithwood, K. (2003) 'Teacher Leadership: Its nature, development and impact on schools and students' in M. Brundrett, N. Burton and R. Smith *Leadership in Education*, London, Sage

Leithwood, K. Jantzi, D. and Steinbach, R. (2003) 'Fostering teacher leadership' in N. Bennett, M. Crawford and M. Cartwright, *Effective Educational Leadership*, London, Paul Chapman

Lingard, B., Hayes, D., Mills, M. and Christie, P. (2003) *Leading Learning*, Maidenhead, Open University Press

Loughran, J. (2010) *What Expert Teachers Do: Enhancing professional knowledge for classroom practice*, London, Routledge

Lumby, J. and Coleman, M. (2007) *Leadership and Diversity: challenging theory and practice in education*, London, Sage

MacBeath J., Gray. J.,Cullen, J., Frost, D., Steward, S. and Swaffield, S. (2007) *Schools on the Edge: Responding to challenging circumstances*, London, Paul Chapman

MacBeath J. and Dempster, N. (eds) (2009) *Connecting Leadership and Learning: Principles for practice*, London, Routledge

Maslow, A. (1954) *Motivation and Personality*, New York, Harper & Row

McGregor, J. (2007) *Developing Thinking, Developing Learning*, Maidenhead, Open University Press

Muijs, D. and Reynolds, D. (2005) *Effective Teaching: Evidence and practice*, London, Sage

Muijs, D. and Harris, A. (2007) 'Teacher leadership in (in) action', *Educational Management, Administration and Leadership* 35, 1: 111–34

O'Donoghue,T. and Clarke, S. (2010) *Leading Learning: Process, themes and issues in international contexts*, London, Routledge

O'Neill, J. (2003) 'Managing through teams' in L. Kydd, L. Anderson and W. Newton, *Leading People and Teams in Education*, London, Paul Chapman.

Pask, R. and Joy, B. (2007) *Mentoring-Coaching: A Guide for Education Professionals*, Maidenhead, Open University Press

Piaget, J. (1950) *The Psychology of Intelligence*, London, Routledge & Kegan Paul

PISA (2006) PISA Results Volume 1 http://www.oecd.org/document/2/0,33 43,en_32252351_32236191_39718850_1_1_1_1,00.html (accessed 10 March 2011)

PISA (2009) PISA Results: What students know and can do: student performance in reading, mathematics and science (volume 1), http://www.oecd.org/document/53/0,37 46,en_32252351_46584327_46584821_1_1_1_1,00.html (accessed 10 March 2011)

QCDA (2009) Personal learning and thinking skills, http://curriculum.qcda.gov.uk/key-stages-3-and-4/skills/ personal-learning-and-thinking-skills/index.aspx (accessed 14 July 2010)

Reber, A.S. (1993) *Implicit Learning and Tacit Knowledge: An essay on the cognitive unconscious*, Oxford, Oxford University Press

Riley, K. (2009) 'Reconfiguring Urban Leadership: A perspective on community', *School Leadership and Management* 29, 1: 51–63

Schmuck, R.A. and Runkel, P.J. (1994) *The Handbook of Organisation Development in Schools and Colleges*, Illinois, Waveland Press

Schon, D. (1983) *The Reflective Practitioner: How professionals think in action*, London, Maurice Temple-Smith

Schon, D. (1987) *Educating the Reflective Practitioner*, San Francisco, Jossey-Bass

Smeets, K. and Ponte, P. (2009) 'Action research and teacher leadership', *Professional Development in Education* 35, 2: 175–93

Southworth, G. (2004) *Primary School Leadership in Context: Leading small, medium and large sized schools*, London, RoutledgeFalmer

Spillane, J.P. (2005) 'Distributed leadership', *The Educational Forum* 69, Winter 2005: 142–50

Stoll, L. and Temperley, J. (2009) 'Creative leadership: a challenge for our times', *School Leadership and Management* 29, 1: 65–78

Sugrue, C. (2009) 'From heroes and heroines to hermaphrodites: emasculation or emancipation of school leaders and leadership?' *School Leadership and Management* 29, 4: 353–71

Swaffield, S. and MacBeath, J. (2009) Chapter 3, 'Leadership for learning' in J. MacBeath and N. Dempster, *Connecting Leadership and Learning: Principles for practice*, London, Routledge

TDA (2007) Professional Standards for Teachers Post-Threshold, http://www.tda.gov.uk/training-provider/

serving-teachers/professional-standards-guidance/~/media/resources/teacher/professional-standards/
standards_postthreshold.pdf (accessed 15 July 2010)

Teaching and Learning Research Programme (TLRP) (2006) 14–19 *Education and Training: A Commentary by the teaching and learning research programme*, TLRP http://www.tlrp.org/pub/documents/14–19%20commentary.pdf (accessed June 23 2010)

Turner, C.K. (2006a) 'Informal learning and its relevance to the early professional development of teachers in secondary schools in England and Wales', *Journal of In-Service Education* 32, 3: 301–19

Turner, C.K. (2006b) 'Subject leaders in secondary schools and informal learning', *School Leadership and Management* 26, 5: 419–35

Turner, C.K. (2009) 'The politics of power in educational middle leadership in secondary schools: a teacher leadership perspective', paper given at the British Educational Research Association (BERA) Annual Conference, Manchester University

Vygotsky, L.S. (1978) *Mind in Society: The development of higher psychological processes*, Cambridge, MA, Harvard University Press

Watkins, C. (2005) *Classrooms as Learning Communities*, London, Routledge.

Watkins, C., Carnell, E. and Lodge, C. (2007) *Effective Learning in Classrooms*, London, Sage

Watkinson, A. (2003) *Managing Teaching Assistants: A guide for headteachers, managers and teachers*, London, RoutledgeFalmer

Webster, R., Blatchford, P., Bassett, P., Brown, P., Martin, C. and Russell, A. (2011) 'The wider pedagogical role of teaching assistants', *School Leadership and Management* 31, 1: 3–20

Wenger, E. (1998) *Communities of Practice: Learning, meaning and identity*, Cambridge, Cambridge University Press

Wilkinson, G. (2005) 'Workforce remodelling and formal knowledge: the erosion of teachers' professional jurisdiction in English schools', *School Leadership and Management* 25, 5: 421–39

Woods, P. (2004) 'Democratic leadership: drawing distinctions with distributed leadership', *International Journal of Leadership in Education* 7, 1: 3–26.

Yin, R.K. (2003) *Case Study Research: Design and methods*, London, Sage, 3rd ed.

Yukl, G. (2008) 'How leaders influence organizational effectiveness', *Leadership Quarterly,* 19, 6: 708–22

Index